DONALD MACLEOD
Princeton Theological Seminary
Princeton, N. J.

DONALD MACLEOD
Princeto   1 Seminary
Princeton, N. J.

THE MEANING
OF
BAPTISM

Books by
JOHN FREDERICK JANSEN
Published by The Westminster Press

Guests of God, *Meditations for the Lord's Supper*
The Meaning of Baptism, *Meditations*

THE MEANING

OF

BAPTISM

Meditations by
JOHN FREDERICK JANSEN

Philadelphia
THE WESTMINSTER PRESS

Library of Congress Catalog Card No. 58–7088

PRINTED IN THE UNITED STATES OF AMERICA

ACKNOWLEDGMENTS

Grateful acknowledgment is made to the following publishers for permission to quote from their copyrighted publications:

Bible: A New Translation, The, by James Moffatt. Copyright, 1922, 1935, 1950, by Harper & Brothers.

Church and the Sacraments, The, by P. T. Forsyth. Independent Press, Limited, 1949.

"For the Time Being, A Christmas Oratorio," in *The Collected Poetry of W. H. Auden.* Copyright, 1944, by W. H. Auden. Random House, Inc.

"Have Thine Own Way, Lord." Hope Publishing Company.

"If Jesus Christ Is a Man," by Richard Gilder. Houghton Mifflin Company.

Letters to Young Churches, translated by J. B. Phillips. The Macmillan Company, 1947.

Man Born to Be King, The, by Dorothy L. Sayers. Harper & Brothers. Copyright, 1943, by Dorothy L. Sayers. Ann Watkins, Inc.

Mrs. Miniver, by Jan Struther. Harcourt, Brace and Company, Inc., 1940.

My Country, by Russell W. Davenport. Copyright, 1944, by Russell W. Davenport. Simon and Schuster, Inc.

Our Faith, by Emil Brunner. Charles Scribner's Sons, 1936.

Parables of Jesus, The, by George Buttrick. Harper & Brothers, 1928.

Point of No Return, by John Marquand. Little, Brown & Co., 1949.

" The Rock," in *Collected Poems, 1909–1935,* by T. S. Eliot. Harcourt, Brace and Company, Inc.

Skin of Our Teeth, The, by Thornton Wilder. Harper & Brothers, 1942.

Strong Name, The, by James Stewart. Charles Scribner's Sons, 1941.

Theology of the Sacraments, The, by Donald Baillie. Charles Scribner's Sons, 1957.

Through Troubled Waters, by William Armstrong. Harper & Brothers, 1957.

TO OUR BOYS

PAUL COLLINS (May 9–10, 1957)
Who Bears the Name There
and
JOHN, TYLER, and MARK
That They May Bear the Name Here

CONTENTS

PREFACE

M AN shall not live by bread alone, but by every word that proceeds from the mouth of God." God's Word is spoken in nature and in history, in creation and in redemption, in word and in sacrament. God's Word is supremely Jesus Christ in whom the world of creation and the world of redemption meet.

If Jesus Christ is the Word of God, then the spoken word is not the whole Word. If the whole Word is to speak to the whole man, Christian faith dare not lose the word that comes in sacrament, for man is not a disembodied spirit but a being of body and spirit. Man lives by symbol and sacrament. He needs every word that proceeds from the mouth of God.

Our rootless age yearns for meaningful symbols, and it is not at all surprising that a lively concern over sacramental life goes on apace in contemporary Christianity. There is a grave and legitimate disquiet about the ambiguous place of the sacraments in the modern church. Sometimes they have become ends in themselves, so that churches have become " efficiently run sacramental filling stations " — as a Catholic churchman has remarked. More often, and especially in modern Protestantism, sacramental practice has become appallingly meaningless and irrelevant.

If these dangers hold true of the Lord's Supper, they are more true of Christian Baptism. Whereas the Protestant sermon seeks to interpret the meaning of the Supper at each observance, one seldom hears Baptism explored or related to the devotional life. All too often infant Baptism is a meaningless social custom instead of a relevant symbol of living faith.

Happily, signs of this disquiet are stirring the church to action, for Biblical study and ecumenical churchmanship are confronting the sacraments in fresh and exciting encounter. The names of Karl Barth and Oscar Cullmann, Frederick W. Dillistone and Paul Tillich, Donald Baillie, W. Flemington, and a host of others come to mind — as well as that pioneer of so much that is contemporary, Peter Taylor Forsyth. Presently the Church of Scotland is restudying the basis of Christian Baptism, and the World Council study groups met at Oberlin in 1957 to seek a fresh distillation of Biblical truth and liturgical practice.

However, this is the task not only of the theologians. It is supremely the task of pulpit and pew to bear relevant witness to the redemptive word of God. This little volume of meditations is addressed to pulpit and pew. It does not presume to be a historical or systematic treatise on the theology of the sacraments or of Baptism in particular. Like its companion piece, *Guests of God* (The Westminster Press, 1956), it aims to be simply and solely a book of meditations. For example, it does not attempt to argue the validity of infant Baptism. It seeks rather to indicate the depths of insight that are part of our reformed and evangelical tradition.

Although these meditations are not sermons, they do wish to make an appeal to the Protestant pulpit. Most of us observe the Lord's Supper at stated times during the church year — and when we do, the sacrament is central, for the whole service interprets and expresses its meaning. Why cannot Baptism be observed at stated times during the church year — and when it is, why cannot it be central instead of an appendage? Might we not learn something from the early church?

These meditations assume that the sacrament of Christian Baptism is itself the enacted word of God, the " text " of each meditation. Scripture passages are not all directly sacramental passages but are chosen for their pictorial quality. Yet I venture to hope that all of them can legitimately point us to that enacted word of God which speaks so eloquently of his love for us and which so movingly knits our response to the measureless grace of God in Jesus Christ, whose name we bear and whose life we share.

BEARING HIS NAME

" I bind unto myself the name,
The strong name of the Trinity."
ST. PATRICK

1

THE OWNER'S MARK

"I bear branded on my body the owner's stamp of the Lord Jesus."

GAL. 6:17 (MOFFATT)

IN THIS moving bit of autobiography the apostle Paul expresses two fundamental insights of Christian faith. The first is that a man is free only when he is the servant of Christ. The second is that a man knows this Lord of his life only through the cross.

Christian freedom is the continuing theme of Paul's letters, and it is the particular theme of this letter to the Galatians. "For freedom Christ has set us free; stand fast therefore, and do not submit again to a yoke of slavery." A Christian man, says Paul, is free from the burden of an impossible summons because he has been welcomed home as a dear child of God and an heir of the eternal Kingdom. Once, he says, "we were slaves to the elemental spirits of the universe." Once we were under the thralldom of sin. Now we are sons. "And because you are sons, God has sent the Spirit of his Son into our hearts, crying, 'Abba! Father!' So through God you are no longer a slave but a son, and if a son then an heir." This is always Paul's answer to those who would distort the good news of a gracious God into a legalism that maintains we have to earn God's love. Paul had once tried that way, and he knew better than any that it was a dead-end street. "O wretched man that I am! Who can deliver me — from myself? " God sets men free!

Freedom! The word speaks eloquently still. We speak of the

" free world "; we cherish our nation as " the home of the free "; we boast of " free enterprise." And yet, what precisely does it mean to be free? In John Marquand's *Point of No Return*, Charlie Gray muses: " What is that line in the Declaration of Independence — or is it the Constitution? ' Life, liberty and the pursuit of happiness.' Well, I suppose everybody's pursuing happiness, and you usually lose your liberty when you do, and the best part of your life. Maybe that's what everything's about. Maybe, I don't know." Charlie Gray is the modern " organization man," whose pretensions of freedom are lost in the conformity of crowd culture. Now, just as freedom has its counterfeits in social and economic life, so it has its counterfeits in religious life. This is why Christian thinkers such as Augustine, Luther, and Calvin depreciated the notion of " free will." They were as concerned as any of us with the reality of responsible selfhood. They only insisted that it is idle to speak of free will unless the will has been freed from the tyrannies of habit and pride and sin. They held — with Paul — that God must set us free — from ourselves. " For freedom Christ has set us free."

Paradoxically, the man who is free knows he is a servant. The same Paul who always maintains the freedom of the Christian man loves to call himself the servant of Jesus Christ, the prisoner of the Lord. In this particular instance Paul is making a last reply to those who want faith to be conformity to a religious system. Rejecting in the name of freedom every other servitude, Paul acknowledges a truer service: " Let no one interfere with me after this, for I bear branded on my body the owner's stamp of the Lord Jesus."

Paul's figure is that of a slave branded with his master's name so that no one can ignore the mark of lordship that is indelibly impressed on him. The figure of speech was not inappropriate to Paul's day when every other man who walked the streets of the capital was a slave. At first sight the figure of speech seems strangely inappropriate to our own day, for we like to think that slavery is a thing of the past. Yet in a deeper sense the language of the apostle is as contemporary as ever, for every man bears

the marks of some lordship. Unless a man is servant of the high-
est he is surely servant to more trivial masteries. " The man who
' does as he likes,' every time he likes," says George Buttrick,
" is slave to his likes, whatever may be his loud pretense of liberty." Henley's boast about being the master of his fate, the captain of his soul, is at best a piteous illusion. A well-known hymn
speaks much more truly:

" Make me a captive, Lord, and then I shall be free;
   Force me to render up my sword, and I shall conqueror be."

This paradoxical truth of freedom in service is witnessed by
every experience of human love, by every expression of fidelity
and honor, and by every growth of personal character. Martin
Luther summed it up in a classic sentence: " A Christian man is
the most free lord of all, and subject to none; a Christian man
is the most dutiful servant of all, and subject to everyone." Says
Paul, " I bear branded on my body the owner's stamp of the
Lord Jesus."

But who is the owner and what are the marks of his lordship?
What are the marks of the Lord Jesus?

Paul knew. The marks of the Lord Jesus are the marks of the
cross. The Lord who claims his life is the Savior who gave his
own life. " You are not your own," Paul writes; " you were
bought with a price." " Far be it from me to glory except in the
cross of our Lord Jesus Christ." I belong to Christ, Paul says,
because he loves me with a love that will not let me go. And
" love so amazing, so divine, demands my soul, my life, my all."

Little wonder, then, that it should become Paul's lifelong de-
sire to know Christ better through the fellowship of his suffering: " Now I rejoice in my sufferings for your sake, and in my
flesh I complete what remains of Christ's afflictions for the sake
of his body, that is, the church." Or again, " I have been crucified with Christ; it is no longer I who live, but Christ who lives
in me; and the life I now live in the flesh I live by faith in the
Son of God, who loved me and gave himself for me." Yes, " I

carry on my scarred body the marks of my Owner, the Lord Jesus" (Phillips).

All this the sacrament of Baptism declares and portrays. In Baptism, God declares me to be his child. In Baptism he welcomes me with the seal of sonship. No hired servant, but the freedom of a father's son! I receive *my* name as I receive *his* name.

On the other hand, Baptism declares that the liberty of sonship is found in the service of love. His name is the owner's mark. That means I am his — not my own. " I carry on my scarred body the marks of my Owner, the Lord Jesus."

Who is the owner? What are his marks? Baptism is a solemn reminder that the Lord of my life is the Savior whose own baptism was of blood. That is why many orders of Christian Baptism portray the owner's mark by making the sign of the cross with the water of baptism.

Baptism is the owner's mark. " I bear branded on my body the owner's stamp of the Lord Jesus." It suggests the only way in which the owner's mark can be worn. " I have been crucified with Christ; and yet I live." That is to say, I bear the owner's mark as I share the owner's concern and learn to live his life in his Spirit. " Let this mind be in you, which was also in Christ Jesus."

> " Hath he marks to lead me to him
>   If he be my Guide?
> ' In his feet and hands are wound prints,
>   And his side.' "

2

THE MARK OF CAIN AND THE MARK OF CHRIST

"And the Lord put a mark on Cain, lest any who came upon him should kill him. Then Cain went away from the presence of the Lord."

GEN. 4:15-16

THE STORY of Cain is a haunting parable in which the terrors of primitive society meet the anxieties of our modern age. Cain has killed his brother and he tries to escape responsibility for breaking the bond of brotherhood with the words, " Am I my brother's keeper?" But there is no escape, for the blood of the slain brother cries aloud to God from the ground, and Cain is cursed. " You shall be a fugitive and a wanderer on the earth." Because the ancient nomad knew no greater terror than to be ostracized from the security of his clan, Cain cries out: " My punishment is greater than I can bear. . . . I shall be a fugitive and a wanderer on the earth, and whoever finds me will slay me." Cain bears the mark of judgment.

The old story has a strange way of bridging the centuries. Our modern world has seen on a more gigantic scale the violation of human brotherhood and, in its wake, a rootless, homeless, anxious humanity. In Thornton Wilder's *The Skin of Our Teeth*, Sabina says to the audience: " As for me, I don't understand a single word of it anyway — all about the troubles the human race has gone through, there's a subject for you. Besides, the author hasn't made up his silly mind as to whether we're all living back in caves or in New Jersey today, and that's the way it is all the way through." The words are ironic, of course, for the playwright has made up his mind clearly enough. He knows that the story of Cain and the mark of Cain are indelibly written across the long centuries. Cain's mother may tell her unhappy son to keep the scar on his forehead covered, but it's no use. " Sometimes I think that it's going away," she says, " and then there it is, just as red as ever." And there is Cain — or Henry or whatever he may call himself today — a homeless fugitive marked for life.

Nonetheless, the Biblical story has a deeper message that is often ignored. The mark that God puts on Cain is not so much the mark of judgment as it is the mark of grace. God puts his mark on Cain not to condemn him but to save him from the violence of retaliatory justice — " lest any who came upon him should kill him." What does this mean? It means that God does not let go of man no matter how sinful and fallen he may be. It means that God does not abandon man to the hell of his own making — to his lostness, wretchedness, fear. It means that the image of God in man, marred and broken as it may be, is not obliterated. It means that God is the kinsman and protector, not only of the murdered man, but also of the murderer! It means that God's mercy and judgment follow us wherever we go.

> " O Lord, thou hast searched me and known me!
>   Thou knowest when I sit down and when I rise up;
>   thou discernest my thoughts from afar.
>   Thou searchest out my path and my lying down,
>   and art acquainted with all my ways. . . .
> " Whither shall I go from thy Spirit?
>   Or whither shall I flee from thy presence?
>   If I ascend to heaven, thou art there!
>   If I make my bed in Sheol, thou art there! "

Yet withal, the story of Cain remains a tragedy. What does he do? " Then Cain went away from the presence of the Lord." Because he fears the blood of the slain brother more than he trusts the Lord of Life, Cain remains a fugitive and a wanderer — estranged from his God, his fellows, and himself. Like Judas, Cain ends in night because he will not face the Lord of Light. When Jesus appealed to Judas at the Supper, Judas, " after receiving the morsel, . . . immediately went out; *and it was night.*" And though the Lord put his mark on Cain, " Cain went away from the presence of the Lord."

Now let the sacrament of Christian Baptism call us from the mark of Cain to the mark of Christ. This mark is similar in setting — but utterly different in its effect!

The mark of Baptism finds man where the mark of Cain also found him — estranged from the beloved community of God, lonely and fearful and guilty. To be baptized is to recognize first of all my need of a cleansing and saving grace.

> " According to thy abundant mercy
>   blot out my transgressions.
>   Wash me thoroughly from my iniquity,
>   and cleanse me from my sin! "

As the Heidelberg Catechism of 1563 put it: " That I am washed with his blood and Spirit from the pollution of my soul, that is, from all my sins, as certainly as I am washed outwardly with water, whereby commonly the filthiness of the body is taken away." There is no place for pride or pretense at Baptism, for all my evasions and alibis are shattered. I am my brother's keeper. In Baptism I confess my lostness and my helplessness. " Wash me thoroughly from my iniquity." The psalmist knew that we are all bound together in the bundle of life:

> " Behold, I was brought forth in iniquity,
>   and in sin did my mother conceive me."

Infant Baptism says this simply and movingly — there are no exceptions to the human problem. We all are in this thing together.

Yet the mark of Christ, as the mark of Cain, is no harsh and inexorable judgment to drive me to despair. It is not the mark of rejection but of acceptance. God has put his mark on me. He will not leave me to myself, for he loves me with a love that will not let me go. His mark is his answer to estrangement and fear. His mark proclaims that he is creating a new community into whose brotherhood I am welcomed. The mark of Christ proclaims eloquently: " You were at that time separated from Christ, alienated from the commonwealth of Israel, and strangers to the covenants of promise, having no hope and without God in the world. But now in Christ Jesus you who once were far off have been brought near in the blood of Christ. . . . So then you are no longer strangers and sojourners, but you are fellow citizens with the saints and members of the household of God."

And what of the mark itself? One wonders what the old story meant by the mark of Cain. Is it meant to be a visible sign, a scarlet letter, an indelible scar? Who knows? What matter? This we know: the mark of Baptism leaves no scar. The washing of water points me, says the old Catechism, to the certainty " that I am washed with his blood." I do not need to bear the deeper scars of that mark, for the scars are his — the Christ of God. He bore the burden of estrangement to give me his fellowship. He suffered the agony of sin's dereliction so that I might have his peace. He died so that I might live. The mark of Christ is seen in the cross of Christ. The mark of Christ proclaims the reality of a redeemed community of God — redeemed by his blood. And Baptism is his mark that welcomes me into that beloved community.

Unhappily Cain fled from community because he thought all others were like himself. This was his hell — quite as dreadfully as the man in Sartre's play, No Exit, who says, " Hell is other people." So Cain remains a fugitive and a stranger because he chooses to live in such isolation. Baptism assures me that there is a better environment. Baptism assures me that I need not flee from God because I need not remain what I am. The gospel declares that all men — including myself — may become more like Christ. " Do you not know," writes Paul, " that all of us who have been baptized into Christ Jesus were baptized into his death? We were buried therefore with him by baptism into death, so that as Christ was raised from the dead by the glory of the Father, we too might walk in newness of life. For if we have been united with him in a death like his, we shall certainly be united with him in a resurrection like his."

Does the mark do this? No, but the Lord who puts his mark on us does this. Neither the mark of Cain nor the mark of Christ will force us magically or mechanically against our will. Said John Calvin: " By these things it is not signified, however, that the water is cause, nor even instrument, of purgation and regeneration, but only that the knowledge of such gifts is received in the sacrament, since we are said to receive, to obtain, and to be appointed to that which we believe to be given by the Lord." Cain could still flee from the presence of the Lord because he did not believe that God meant what he signified in his mark.

But why should we flee? " Lord, to whom shall we go? You have the words of eternal life." In Baptism we believe that God means what his mark says. That is the saving difference between the mark of Christ and the mark of Cain.

> " Abel's blood for vengeance
> Pleaded to the skies;
> But the blood of Jesus
> For our pardon cries."

3

WHOSE NAME DO YOU BEAR?

" And I saw a beast rising out of the sea . . . and a blasphemous name. . . . Also it causes all, . . . both rich and poor, both free and slave, to be marked on the right hand or the forehead, so that no one can buy or sell unless he has the mark, that is, the name of the beast or the number of its name."

REV. 13:1, 16-17

" Then I looked, and lo, on Mount Zion stood the Lamb, and with him a hundred and forty-four thousand who had his name and his Father's name written on their foreheads."

REV. 14:1

IN that strange and haunting vision which is the book of Revelation, the seer of Patmost expresses a truth of tremendous moment. To be sure, Jesus had said long before that " no one can serve two masters," but for John this truth assumes cosmic proportions as he envisions the ultimate destinies of mankind On the one hand, he sees a vast host who follow the Beast from the abyss and who bear his name. On the other hand, he sees the multitude of the redeemed, who stand with the Lamb on Mt. Zion and who bear on their foreheads the name of the Lamb and the name of God. The meaning is clear. Every man is a marked man. In the conflict of ultimate loyalties there is no middle way. Every man bears the mark of the Beast or the mark of the Lamb.

" And the choice goes on forever 'twixt that darkness and that
    light."

Is this apocalyptic vision exaggerated or is it sober truth? Our time is apt to seek life's meaning either in individualism or in collectivism, but John's vision knows that the answer does not lie in either direction, for life has deeper dimensions.

The Word of God knows that a rampant individualism does not adequately interpret human life. No man is an island, for we are bound together in the bundle of life. No man can stand alone, for we are members one of another. It is a significant fact that the Hebrews were aware of corporate selfhood and corporate responsibility long before they were concerned with individual immortality. They knew that " third and fourth generations " are touched by what we do. This is a fundamental note in the Christian gospel — salvation and damnation are never merely private concerns. There is a Kingdom of God and there is a kingdom of evil.

However, although life's meaning cannot be found in rampant individualism, neither is it found in collective conformity. Ours is the age of " crowd culture," where the individual seeks anonymity in the group. Yet the judgment of God never allows us to escape personal accountability. Two shall be in the field, said Jesus; one shall be taken and the other left. John may see two vast companies of mankind, but each of these is made up of individual faces and each forehead bears the mark of its master.

What shall we say of the Beast and the Lamb? Can we take such imagery seriously? What especially shall we say of the Beast? That men in ancient times believed in a power of evil — a devil and his legions — all this is true enough. It is plain that Jesus thought of life as a cosmic battlefield where the Kingdom of God hurls back the kingdom of Satan. It is evident that Paul shared this view that " we are not contending against flesh and blood, but against principalities, against the powers, against the world rulers of this present darkness, against the spiritual hosts of wickedness in the heavenly places." Well and good, but can we moderns believe that?

Paradoxically, our time is rediscovering the devil — not a cartooned devil with horns and a pitchfork, of course, for that was never the devil of vital experience. We are rather learning afresh what the devil means — that the dimension of evil and the mystery of evil and the scope of evil defy all surface explanations. Is there any better way of saying what must be said about the depth of evil than to say that the Beast comes from the abyss? This is truer insight than all facile attempts to resolve the problem of evil. The Beast comes from the abyss, from the unknown and the unknowable — but the Beast is real enough.

John saw the Beast with ten horns and seven heads, with ten diadems and a blasphemous name. Our time has seen the Beast with many more heads and myriad horns but still bearing the blasphemous name and clutching the diadems that belong to God. One head is that brutal, sinister face men saw in the concentration camps of Buchenwald and Dachau. Little wonder that Hermann Rauschning's book about Hitler was titled *The Beast from the Abyss.* Another head is that smiling but still demonic face that speaks of a brotherhood of man while scorning the sanctity of human life. A more familiar face is that secular materialism seen in a hundred different poses on the blatant billboards of our sensate culture. Multitudes may hail this machine face as God, but Russell Davenport sees what it is in a poem that sums up the greatness and the poverty of our time. What happens to men, he asks, when they believe in machines but not in ultimate meaning?

> " We have found Nothing:
> We have seen it, have
> Seen Nothing — the face
> Of Nothing — we know
> Nothing, we have heard
> Nothing, heard it rant,
> Heard it proclaim the
> New Order of Hate,
> The Godless Order:
> The radio face
> In the darkness of hate

> Where man ends who
> Is without freedom,
> Is the machine-man,
> The instrument-man,
> The automatic
> Man without soul — where
> Man is without God:
> Not God's face, not God's
> Face, but man's — man's face,
> The man-face without
> Love, the machine-face,
> The instrument-face
> Without faith without
> Hope — man's face without
> Christ, the Anti-Christ."

The Beast still comes from the abyss.

But the Lamb comes from Mt. Zion! John knows that the name of the Lamb is stronger than the name of the Beast. He knows that those who bear the mark of the Lamb shall vanquish those who bear the mark of the Beast. History is not a hopeless fatality, for the Beast shall not have the last word. The vision of the Beast and his followers provides the foil and contrast by which the seer comes to the saving word about human destiny. "Then I looked, and lo, on Mount Zion stood the Lamb." The Lamb is mightier than the Beast. While the Beast strives desperately to clutch to his stolen diadems, the Lamb who had died is given a name above every name. " Behold, the Lamb of God, who takes away the sin of the world! " Because the Lamb has done this he holds the future and receives the throne of the universe. The vision of the throne declares that God is almighty. The vision of the Lamb declares that God is almighty in his love. Power and pardon meet, for the Lord of Life is the Lamb who was slain!

> " Crown him with many crowns,
> The Lamb upon his throne."

The Lamb does not stand alone. With him are the hundred and forty-four thousand who bear his name and his Father's name. At other moments in John's vision this company becomes " a great multitude which no man could number, from every nation, from all tribes and peoples and tongues, standing before the throne and before the Lamb." The Lamb does not stand alone, for his people bear his name in their foreheads. That means, of course, that I do not stand alone if I bear his name.

> " None other Lamb, none other name,
>   None other Hope in heaven or earth or sea,
>   None other Hiding Place from guilt and shame,
>   None beside thee."

So John sees that the ultimate truth about human destiny is not with those who deny God but with those " who had conquered the beast and its image and the number of its name, standing beside the sea of glass with harps of God in their hands. And they sing . . . the song of the Lamb." What a picture! The corridors of heaven are ringing with the song of the redeemed!

If this vision still seems remote and unattainable, let the sacrament of Baptism portray it in tangible sign and symbol.

In the first place, Christian Baptism is God's answer to our extremes of individualism and collectivism. As a covenant sign, Baptism declares that God creates a new people for himself. God is not interested in saving scattered individuals without knitting them into a beloved community. This is precisely why we believe that infant Baptism is a valid expression of this sacramental truth. God's promise is to us and to our children, binding us all together in the covenant of his love. At Baptism the congregation is sponsor and participant. Baptism is never a private ritual but a sacrament of the worshiping community of God's people.

At the same time, the act of Baptism does not forget that in this community of faith there is no substitute for personal response. Each member of God's people bears the name of the Lamb on his forehead and for that reason becomes personally responsible to bear that name faithfully. The outward act of Baptism must become an inward experience. It is not enough for our names to be written on the church register unless they are also written in the Lamb's book of life.

Moreover, Baptism points dramatically to the deeper dimensions of our life. It reminds us that unless we bear the mark of the Lamb we bear the mark of the Beast. We do not believe, as some do, that the act of Baptism itself removes the stains of sin, but we do believe that life is an ultimate either-or. Baptism declares that there are two realms, two peoples, two destinies. In Baptism we rejoice that " he has delivered us from the dominion of darkness and transferred us to the kingdom of his beloved Son, in whom we have redemption, the forgiveness of sins." We can rejoice that we may stand with the Lamb on Mt. Zion. A Lutheran baptismal service portrays this effectively when it reads: " Let us now hear the renunciation and confess the faith into which we baptize our children: I renounce the devil, all his works, and all his ways. I believe in God, the Father Almighty. . . . I believe in Jesus Christ. . . . I believe in the Holy Ghost. . . ." Is this not a sacramental counterpart to the vision John had on Patmos?

Let us take the vision and the sacrament seriously. Every man is a marked man, for every man bears the name of some mastery. Whose name do we bear? Christian Baptism offers us the name of the Lamb. Sacrament and vision and experience unite to say:

> " The tide of time shall never
> His covenant remove;
> His name shall stand forever —
> That name to us is Love."

4

"THE NAME ALL VICTORIOUS"

" He who conquers, I will make him a pillar in the temple of my God; never shall he go out of it, and I will write on him the name of my God, and the name of the city of my God, the New Jerusalem which comes down from my God out of heaven, and my own new name."

Rev. 3:12

M AN LIVES in two worlds," writes H. Richard Niebuhr, "and when he tries to make his home in one alone something goes wrong with him. Our race, like that of the migratory birds, cannot live and perform all its functions in one climate but must undertake a periodic flight to another homeland." Too often we forget this. Some try to live wholly in the world of time; others try to escape wholly into the world of eternity. The gospel, on the other hand, " always carries with it the double injunction to seek the things that are above and to go into all the world. Yet it does not consist of two proclamations, for it speaks of one God who redeems a life lived in two worlds." The gospel of the incarnation declares that God has come into time to save this world. The gospel of the resurrection declares that the realm beyond our sight will also be transformed into a realm of grace and glory.

This insight is not new. The writer of the book of Revelation lived in its awareness, for he was able to live life on two levels. Over one environment he had no control. " I . . . was on the island called Patmos," where concentration camp was stark

reminder of a world of evil. He had, however, another environment which no outward circumstances could take from him. " I
was in the Spirit on the Lord's day." Because he lived in the
dimension of eternity as well as of time, John could see beyond
the limits of the temporal to the goal of all time and to the
very meaning of existence. Accordingly, when the Christ who is
both the beginning and the end bids him write to the churches,
John sees present and future woven into one glorious reality.
He hears the Lord of Life say, " He who conquers, I will make
him a pillar in the temple of my God; never shall he go out of
it, and I will write on him the name of my God, and the name
of the city of my God, the New Jerusalem which comes down
from my God out of heaven, and my own new name."

Think what that means to those whose lives are hard pressed
in the battle of life! The Christ who could say as he faced his
own cross, " Be of good cheer, I have overcome the world," tells
his followers that they can conquer too. That is why Jesus Christ
is the great contemporary of all who fight manfully against
evil, " afflicted in every way, but not crushed; perplexed, but
not driven to despair."

Christ promises his followers that they shall be pillars in the
temple of his God. Pillars are permanent, and God's people will
always be with their God. Is this not our deepest yearning?

> " One thing have I asked of the Lord,
>   that will I seek after;
> that I may dwell in the house of the Lord
>   all the days of my life,
> to behold the beauty of the Lord,
>   and to inquire in his temple."

Can we be sure of God's promise? All of us have moments of
aching uncertainty when we wonder if the struggle is worth-
while.

> " Say not the struggle naught availeth,
>   The labor and the wounds are vain,

The enemy faints not, nor faileth,
And as things have been they remain."

Is there some reassuring word? Such a word must come to us
sub specie aeternitatis — if we can see the present in the light
of eternity. John's vision is not conjured up to satisfy some idle
curiosity or to provide some dream-world escape. The man who
caught this vision was able to live triumphantly today because he
was sure of tomorrow. You and I stand with him in a world of
tragedy and fear. Can we not also stand with him in the dimension of eternity? Does the Voice he heard not speak as
clearly today? " He who conquers, I will make him a pillar in the
temple of my God; never shall he go out of it." Is this not the
selfsame voice of Christ, " Come, O blessed of my Father, in-
herit the kingdom prepared for you from the foundation of the
world "? Is he not the same yesterday, today, and forever?

" Thou wast their Rock, their Fortress, and their Might;
Thou, Lord, their Captain in the well-fought fight;
Thou, in the darkness drear, their one true Light. Alleluia."

What is the badge of this victory? " I will write on him the
name of my God, and the name of the city of my God . . . and
my own new name." In Biblical thought, of course, the name of
God is always God's revealed character: " The name of the Lord
is a strong tower; the righteous man runs into it and is safe."
God's name is God himself — God revealed in word and act. " A
mighty Fortress is our God." To be sure of God we need no
other credential than his name.

John hears the name as a threefold name. " The name of my
God." In the priestly benediction of the Old Testament, the
familiar words, " The Lord bless you and keep you . . ." are
followed by the words, " So shall they put my name upon the
people . . . and I will bless them." God and his people are
bound together in an everlasting covenant.

" And the name of the city of my God." God's name welcomes us to God's people and to God's sanctuary. To bear the

name of the city of God is to be acknowledged as one of its citizens. " Our commonwealth is in heaven," writes Paul, " and from it we await a Savior, the Lord Jesus Christ." And what is this communion of saints if not an expression of the communion of the Holy Spirit?

" And my own new name." Always the climatic name through which we know the whole name of God is the name of Jesus Christ. " Take the name of Jesus with you! " Here it is " the new name " to indicate the Christian's confidence that the name of Jesus is " the name, all victorious, . . . [whose] Kingdom is glorious, and rules over all." What name, indeed, shall we not give to him whose name is above every name? And how shall this name be known if not in the hearts and lives of his church?

> " Through her shall every land proclaim
> The sacred might of Jesus' name."

John's vision is true. We are children of two worlds, and our attempt to live in one world is an escape from reality. This is the burden of Dr. Niebuhr's plea for a new otherworldliness. However, the trouble with most of our preoccupations with the other world, he says, is that " they remain too largely movements of thought, unaccompanied by those active demonstrations of faith in the reality of the unseen which give the thinker assurance that he is not deceiving himself with abstractions."

The sacrament of Baptism can help us here, for it is an " active demonstration of faith in the reality of the unseen." The visible deed on earth can link us with the invisible deed in heaven. What happens in time can point us to what happens in eternity. God made heaven *and* earth, and earth is not too remote from heaven to point us to the eternal. This Baptism knows: " Set apart this water from a common to a sacred use, and grant that what we now do on earth may be confirmed in heaven."

Moreover, Baptism enjoins a task as it claims a promise. It asks God's help that we may conquer. In infant Baptism we pray, " Bring him safely through the perils of childhood, deliver

him from the temptations of youth, and lead him to witness a
good confession, and to persevere therein to the end." Nor is it
different with the Baptism of adults: " Defend, O Lord, this thy
servant with thy heavenly grace; that he may continue thine for
ever; and daily increase in thy Holy Spirit more and more, until
he come unto thine everlasting kingdom."

In Baptism we are given the triune name of God — " in the
name of the Father, and of the Son, and of the Holy Ghost." We
know the name of the Father and the Spirit because we know
the Son. That is why the earliest formula of Baptism was simply
" in the name of the Lord Jesus." The doctrine of the Trinity
which becomes the baptismal formula is only that view of God
made necessary by what we believe and know about Jesus Christ.
In Jesus Christ the name of God becomes fully known. That is
why his name is ever new:

> " The Joy of all who dwell above,
>   The Joy of all below
> To whom he manifests his love,
>   And grants his name to know."

As the vision of eternity is social, so is the sign on earth. Be-
lievers are given the name of the city of their God and are welcomed into its commonwealth. " This child is now received into
Christ's church: and you the people of this congregation in receiving this child promise with God's help to be his sponsor to
the end that he may confess Christ as his Lord and Savior and
come at last to his eternal kingdom."

" And come at last to his eternal kingdom." The seal of Baptism is a tangible expression of the vision of eternity. " He who
conquers, I will make him a pillar in the temple of my God . . .
and I will write on him . . . the name of the city of my God,
the New Jerusalem which comes down from my God out of
heaven." The city must come from heaven, for earth cannot of
itself produce it. Once again, vision and sacrament remind us
that this Kingdom does not come with observation; " nor will
they say, ' Lo, here it is! ' or ' There! ' for behold, the kingdom

of God is in the midst of you." It is here — and it is there — for he who meets us every day will meet us at the end.

He can give us his new name, for he says, " Behold, I make all things new." He can make us new. " All hail the power of Jesus' name! "

5

KNOWING IN PART — KNOWN IN FULL

" I call you by your name, I surname you, though you do not know me."

Isa. 45:4

" Now I know in part; but then shall I know even as also I am known."

I Cor. 13:12

BAPTISM — especially infant Baptism — raises a difficult question. When a baby is baptized and is " received into Christ's church," does that make any difference to the child? Some say it is primarily an act of dedication on the part of parent and church, but the sacrament says it is primarily an act on God's part. How can this be? Does Baptism make the child's salvation automatic? Surely not! The child, as each of us, must come to his own personal decision of faith, and neither parent nor church can make this decision for him. Baptism is not magic. Well, then, does Baptism only express a fond parental hope? To this again we say, Surely not! Baptism expresses God's will — not just the will of parent or church. How can this be? How can Baptism be something other than magical or meaningless? This is the question of Christian Baptism.

The sacrament, of course, only raises the deeper question of life itself. Sacrament and Word both point me to the mystery of life under God. As the psalmist expressed it:

" For thou didst form my inward parts,
       thou didst knit me together in my mother's womb. . . .
    Thy eyes beheld my unformed substance;
       in thy book were written, every one of them,
    the days that were formed for me,
       when as yet there was none of them."

"We do not just happen to exist," says Emil Brunner. "Although we were begotten and born of our parents, we come from
eternity, from the eternal thought and will of God. . . . Deep,
deep are the roots of our life. Far beyond all temporal visibility,
it roots in the divine invisibility, in the eternal ' counsels.' "

This depth, this eternal dimension of our life, is what theology
seeks to express in its doctrine of election or predestination.
This doctrine does not intend to become a playground for
curiosity and speculation. It will never reduce to a nice formula
that explains why everything happens that does happen. It wants
to say one thing only — " deep, deep are the roots of my life."

Is it important to say this? Simply put, it means that if our
origin lies in God's purpose, our destiny lies there also. " When
a man is permitted to perceive that God sees him from eternity,"
says Brunner, " when the eternally beholding eyes of God rest
upon him and his view meets God's eternal vision, the greatest
thing that can happen on earth transpires. A man then knows
that God loves him *from* eternity and *for* eternity. God has
chosen me from eternity to eternity. That is the faith, the full,
whole, evangelical faith — election from eternity." This, after
all, is only to say what the whole New Testament says: "We
love [him], because he first loved us."

In a hundred different ways the Word of God points us to this
deeper dimension of life. When Moses stood perplexed and
troubled by events he could neither comprehend nor control, he
cried out: " Yet thou hast said, ' I know you by name, and you
have found favor in my sight.' Now therefore, I pray thee, if I
have found favor in thy sight, show me now thy ways, that I
may know thee." When young Samuel first heard the voice of

God we read that he " did not yet know the Lord." When young
Jeremiah was called he heard God say:

> " Before I formed you in the womb I knew you,
>   and before you were born I consecrated you."

So Jesus said to his disciples, " You did not choose me, but I
chose you," while to all his followers he says still, " I know my
sheep."

God knows us " by name." He sees us, seeks us, saves us as
persons. We are never statistics to God. This awareness is basic
not only to a sense of salvation but to a true sense of vocation.
Minister and missionary are not the only persons " called " by
God. Every man's life is to be a plan of God. This truth was
recognized by the great prophet of the exile, himself unknown,
when he described the career of Cyrus the Persian. On the face
of it, he says, Cyrus appears to be the master of history. But, if
God is the Lord, history is his story. Therefore God says to
Cyrus:

> " Thus says the Lord to his anointed, to Cyrus,
>   whose right hand I have grasped, . . .
> that you may know that it is I, the Lord,
>   the God of Israel, who call you by your name. . . .
> I call you by your name,
>   I surname you, though you do not know me."

Always it is so. Unseen and unrecognized as he may be, God is
in our midst, and the clue to life lies in recognizing him. As
John the Baptist cried, " I baptize with water; but among you
stands one whom you do not know."

" Whom you do not know." But he knows you! This is the
deepest and truest insight of living faith. After all, if the whole
issue of faith depended on our knowing him, who of us dares
stand? The same Peter who in one glorious moment can say,
" We have believed, and have come to know, that you are the
Holy One of God," is the same man who in a moment of weak-

ness can say, " I know him not." In plain fact, our poor faith is
not enough, and to trust ourselves is to court catastrophe. That
is why Jesus warns the Seventy, " Nevertheless do not rejoice in
this, that the spirits are subject to you; but rejoice that your
names are written in heaven." When all is said and done, Paul
speaks for us all: " For now we see through a glass, darkly; but
then face to face: now I know in part; but then shall I know
even as also I am known."

This is the saving antidote to despair. " Lord," cried Peter,
" you know everything; you know that I love you." If, in some
dark night of the soul, I cry out, " Oh, that I knew where I might
find him! " I can remember that " thou hast searched me and
known me! "

Such faith does not make me passive or complacent with what
I am. " Now I know in part; but then shall I know even as also
I am known " — so Paul's lifelong goal is to " know him." Jesus
prayed for his followers " that they may know thee the only true
God, and Jesus Christ whom thou hast sent. . . . Holy Father,
keep them in thy name which thou hast given me, that they
may be one, even as we are one . . . so that the world may
know that thou hast sent me and hast loved them even as thou
hast loved me. . . . I made known to them thy name, and I
will make it known, that the love with which thou hast loved
me may be in them, and I in them."

Thus the Word of God points me to the deeper roots of my
life, not for the sake of speculative curiosity, but for the sake of
an adequate trust in God.

Now, if the Word points me to such a God, shall not the visi-
bly enacted word in Baptism point me to the same God? And is
this not precisely what Baptism does say? The sacrament declares that God has known me long before I knew him. It declares that God knew my name long before I knew his name.
Baptism assures me that God has given me his name, so that I
may come to know even as also I am known.

Shall the doctrine of election frighten or disturb me? Is it not
rather a saving and steadying conviction that my life is hid in

God, and that " God's firm foundation stands, bearing this seal:
' The Lord knows those who are his ' "?

Would you prefer it the other way? Would you prefer a God
who would say to you, " I never knew you; depart from me "?
Let us be grateful that Word and sacrament speak otherwise.
" So we know and believe the love God has for us. . . . And
we know that the Son of God has come and has given us understanding, to know him who is true; and we are in him who is
true, in his Son Jesus Christ. This is the true God and eternal
life."

Yes, this is the true God to whom in Baptism we give ourselves and our children. This is eternal life, for although we but
know in part, he knows us from everlasting to everlasting.

6

YOUR NEW NAME

"Jesus looked at him, and said, 'So you are Simon the son of John? You shall be called Cephas' (which means Peter)."

JOHN 1:42

"Therefore, if any one is in Christ, he is a new creation; the old has passed away, behold, the new has come."

II COR. 5:17

CHRISTIAN BAPTISM is concerned with God's name and with your name. What's in a name? Biblical thought would say that everything is in a name, for one's name is the revelation of one's character.

This is supremely true of God's name. "Those who know thy name put their trust in thee," the psalmist sings. To know God's name is to be sure of God. In Old Testament times, for example, God is known as "Yahweh" — the great "I Am," the Eternal. He is known as "the God of Abraham and of Isaac and of Jacob" — the God of personal fellowship and covenant promise. He is known as "the God of Israel" — the God of history whose purpose controls and redeems the course of events. Holy history always begins when "men began to call upon the name of the Lord." In the New Testament the purpose of God finds its fulfillment in Jesus Christ. "You shall call his name Jesus, for he will save his people from their sins." God gives Jesus "the name which is above every name." Throughout the Bible the name of God is the basis for men's confidence in God. "The Lord is my

43

shepherd. . . . He leads me . . . for his name's sake." Therefore, to make light of God's name is to make light of God: " You
shall not take the name of the Lord your God in vain." Christian
Baptism is Christian faith calling upon the name of the Lord.

Baptism, however, is also concerned with your name — and
mine. " What is the Christian name of this child? " Well, what's
in a name? Just as the Bible is careful to safeguard the name of
God, so it is also concerned to safeguard each person's name.
" You shall not bear false witness against your neighbor." A
person's name is the seal of individual selfhood and personal dig-
nity. " A good name is to be chosen rather than great riches."
Shakespeare puts the same truth in familiar lines:

" Good name in man and woman, dear my lord,
   Is the immediate jewel of their souls.
   Who steals my purse steals trash; 'tis something, nothing;
   'Twas mine, 'tis his, and has been slave to thousands;
   But he that filches from me my good name
   Robs me of that which not enriches him,
   And makes me poor indeed."

Everything is in a name. That is why the men of the Bible
paid such particular attention to choosing the right name for
their children. The prophets often give their children symbolic
names, and the hope of the future becomes enshrined in the
Messiah's name:

" And his name will be called
   ' Wonderful Counselor, Mighty God,
      Everlasting Father, Prince of Peace.' "

Indeed, whenever a man in the Old Testament carries the letters
" el " or " Je " in his name he is carrying the name of God in
promise and in hope. Naming a child was serious business in
Biblical times. It still is, though we are less bound by custom
and tradition and often more intent on pleasing sound and
syllable than aware of a name's meaning. How many would

recognize, for example, that " Irene " means " peace," or that " John " means " God's messenger "? Yet names still carry symbolic strength. Need we remind ourselves that Iosif Vissarionovich Dzhugashvili took the name " Stalin " because he wanted to be known as a " man of steel "?

Because so much is in a name, the Bible often portrays a transformation of character through a change of name. The classic example in the Old Testament is the story of Jacob (" usurper "). Jacob had long tried to live life on his own terms — he had lied, cheated, and dissembled. But there came a time when he reached the end of that road, and one night he faced the future lonely and afraid. Then, says the old story, Jacob met God in mystic and transforming encounter. " And Jacob was left alone; and a man wrestled with him until the breaking of the day." From that shattering and saving experience the once arrogant Jacob came away limping — " a broken and contrite heart." Jacob now knows that he cannot go on alone. " I will not let you go, unless you bless me." " What is your name? " the other asks. " And he said, ' Jacob.' . . . ' Your name shall no more be called Jacob, but Israel [God strives], for you have striven with God and with men, and have prevailed.' " When Jacob asks the other, " Tell me, I pray, your name," no answer is needed, for Jacob trembles in the knowledge that the Almighty has not obliterated him. " I have seen God face to face, and yet my life is preserved." Indeed, it is precisely *because* he has seen God face to face that his life is preserved. So Jacob becomes Israel, the friend and servant of God. The end of Jacob is the beginning of Israel. The old story is ever new: " For all that is in the world, the lust of the flesh and the lust of the eyes and the pride of life, is not of the Father but is of the world. And the world passes away, and the lust of it; but he who does the will of God abides for ever."

The classic example in the New Testament is Simon Peter. " Jesus looked at him, and said, ' So you are Simon the son of John? You shall be called Cephas (which means Peter [rock]).' " If Jacob was an unlikely prospect for sainthood, so was Simon.

Well-meaning but unstable Simon — what can Jesus see in him — or in me?

> " All I could never be,
> All, men ignored in me,
> This, I was worth to God."
> — *Robert Browning*.

This is the good news of faith. Christ sees more in me than others see — or than I can see. " So you are Simon the son of John? You shall be . . . Peter." " You are Peter, and on this rock I will build my church." What amazing confidence the Lord of Life has in us! What astonishing things he can do with us! To " as many as received him, to them gave he power to become . . ."

This, Baptism declares. To be sure, the sacrament leaves many questions unanswered. When and how does it happen? Does it happen in the act of Baptism? Do I become a new man when I am baptized, or am I baptized because I have been made a new man? Or does the promise of Baptism wait for some future confirmation? On such questions Christian views of Baptism have not agreed.

Perhaps we shall never know. Perhaps no stereotyped process is possible. For that matter, it is interesting to observe that the Gospels do not make it plain exactly when Simon received his new name. The Fourth Gospel suggests that he received the name when he first met Jesus. Luke suggests that he received the name when he was chosen one of the Twelve, while Matthew suggests that he received the name when he made his great confession of faith. Evidently the early church felt a similar uncertainty about Baptism. In The Acts, the transforming Spirit is described sometimes as coming to people prior to Baptism, sometimes attendant with Baptism, and sometimes after Baptism. It is a wholesome reminder that we may not stereotype the working of the Spirit of God in human life. The Spirit is like the wind, said Jesus, and it " blows where it wills," and we know not " whence it comes or whither it goes."

What matters is not so much *when* it happens as *that* it happens. The Westminster Confession of Faith recognized this in the following words: " The efficacy of Baptism is not tied to that moment of time wherein it is administered; yet, notwithstanding, by the right use of this ordinance the grace promised is not only offered, but really exhibited and conferred by the Holy Ghost, to such (whether of age or infants) as that grace belongeth unto, according to the counsel of God's own will, in his appointed time."

Certainly the new name does not mean the end of struggle. The old Jacob does not die easily and the old Simon reasserts himself time and again in tragic failures of the spirit. That is why our Reformation fathers used to speak of " *simul sanctus, simul peccator* " — saint and sinner at the same time! And that is why the church is both " holy catholic " and a not-so-holy and not-so-united company of sinners.

However, although Simon Peter may still forget his Lord, this Lord who has called Simon to become Peter does not forget him. " Simon, Simon, . . . I have prayed for you that your faith may not fail." Once again we are confronted with the Love that will not let us go. " I am sure," says Paul, " that he who began a good work in you will bring it to completion at the day of Jesus Christ." Baptism declares that although I have not always looked to him, he has always looked at me.

What, then, will you do with your name? There were two disciples named Judas. The name itself is honorable, for it derives from that tribe that had enshrined the glory and hope of Israel. The name was honorable, but one man made it forever a badge of shame. This is a sober warning for each of us and for the church. There is no greater tragedy than the judgment of the Lord: " I know your works; you have the name of being alive, and you are dead."

All this suggests that we need a stronger name than our own. Whose name? The Roman tradition always adds the name of a patron saint in Baptism, so that the person baptized may imitate the saint's virtues and claim his protection. In itself, of course, there is nothing amiss in linking oneself with the stalwarts of faith and expressing in this fashion the steadying sense of the communion of saints. This is but to remember that "others have labored," and we have "entered into their labor." Many a Protestant loves to carry the name of Peter or Paul or Calvin or Luther or Wesley.

Yet only one name is protector. That is why we cannot rely on "patron" saints. Only one name can save and sanctify. No other can — no other is needed:

> "None other Lamb, none other name,
>> None other Hope in heaven or earth or sea,
> None other Hiding Place from guilt and shame,
>> None beside thee."

Simon Peter knew that. From personal experience he knew that Christ alone could raise the fallen. Pointing to a man who had been lame, he cries, "And his name, by faith in his name, has made this man strong whom you see and know." "There is no other name under heaven given among men by which we must be saved."

All this, Christian Baptism declares. With the struggling saints of all ages Christian parents can say:

> "May he grant you your heart's desire,
>> and fulfill all your plans!
> May we shout for joy over your victory,
>> and in the name of our God set up our banners!"

For the God of Jacob is the God and Father of our Lord Jesus Christ. "He gives power to the faint, and to him who has no might he increases strength."

SHARING HIS DEATH

" I bind my heart this tide
  To the Galilean's side,
  To the wounds of Calvary,
  To the Christ who died for me."
    LAUCHLAN MACLEAN WATT

7

BAPTISM OF BLOOD

" In those days Jesus came from Nazareth of Galilee and was baptized by John in the Jordan."

MARK 1:9.

" I have a baptism to undergo — what tension I suffer, till it is all over! "

LUKE 12:50 (MOFFATT)

" One of the soldiers pierced his side with a spear, and at once there came out blood and water."

JOHN 19:34

O UR PROTESTANT VIEW of the sacraments finds a vivid portrayal in the Fourth Gospel's description of Christ's death. " One of the soldiers pierced his side with a spear, and at once there came out blood and water. He who saw it has borne witness — his testimony is true, and he knows that he tells the truth — that you also may believe."

What does the Evangelist see? He sees the whole drama of salvation expressed in the event of the cross. He sees the cross not only as an event in the past but also as *the* event that shapes the present. He sees the atoning death of the Savior continually expressed in the sacraments of the church. He sees that Word and sacrament bear witness together that our life is through Christ's death.

" Let the water and the blood,
From thy riven side which flowed,
Be of sin the double cure,
Cleanse me from its guilt and power."

" Our sacraments," said Augustine, " have flowed from Christ's side." This description of the crucifixion is not so much a medical report as it is a meaningful sacramental sign — " that you also may believe."

What is a sacrament? It is an unhappy fact that Christians cannot agree as to the number and the meaning of the sacraments. Two Christian traditions insist that seven sacraments link all the stages of life's pilgrimage to the grace of God. They insist, moreover, that without such sacramental and priestly mediation the grace of God is not given.

To this we must say no. Although we gladly recognize a " sacramental universe " in which creation everywhere bears the marks of its Lord, we insist that the sacraments of Christian worship are rooted in history — in the history of redemption. Sacraments do not add anything to God's word of gracious love; they are signs and seals of that word. Sacraments are the enacted word of God proclaiming Christ crucified. Only Baptism and the Supper are directly instituted by Christ himself. Only Baptism and the Supper bring us directly to the event of his cross.

" Let the water and the blood, from thy riven side " do this. Let us remember that water as well as blood flowed from the riven side. Failure to do this has made Baptism a much less meaningful symbol than the Supper. When the water of Baptism is separated from the blood of the cross, attention wanders from Christ to the beauty of the baby or to the faith of the parents or to the skill of the minister — to everything except to the grace of Christ. What? asks Paul. " Was Paul crucified for you? Or were you baptized in the name of Paul? " No, no. " We preach Christ crucified."

Water and blood. Water is the symbol of birth. Modern depth psychology is showing us how pervasive is this archetypal imagery, and is giving new meaning to Jesus' words that we are born " of water and the Spirit." Blood is life given — death. Yet birth and death are not so far apart as we sometimes think. Birth and death meet in Matthew's story of the Nativity. Birth and death meet in the Passion.

Baptism declares that he who makes all things new has made us new — therefore Baptism is not repeated. The Supper declares that he who has begun a good work in us will complete it — therefore the Supper is continually repeated as we are nourished and sustained by him. Both declare that newness of life is not a mere possibility but a divinely given reality. Both declare that we may have his life because he has borne our death. So the two sacraments portray the word that " he has reconciled us . . . to God in one body through the cross." In the sacraments each of us can say, " I do see, I do witness, I do believe." Both in the water and the blood

> " Mine eye at times can see
> The very dying form of One
> Who suffered there for me."

Jesus began his ministry by being baptized by John in the Jordan. Why? Was he another sinner needing forgiveness? Then he cannot help me. Is it appropriate that the Son of God should be baptized as a sinner? The question troubled the early church, and Matthew's Gospel suggests that the Baptist himself protested, saying, " I need to be baptized by you." Think of it! The Son of God baptized as a sinner!

Yet Jesus was baptized, and he saw the heavens opened and heard a Voice declaring, " Thou art my beloved Son; with thee I am well pleased." For Jesus this baptism was his call. In his baptism he knew that the Messiah must become the Servant, " numbered with the transgressors." That is why Jesus begins his ministry with an Ash Wednesday and a Lenten season. In her play, Dorothy Sayers pictures Jesus returning to tell John what the baptismal experience meant to him. " I felt the shoulders of God stoop under the weight of man's sin. And I knew — . . . I knew what it meant to be the Son of Man."

This is why Jesus' own baptism in the Jordan was of such decisive importance to him. It pointed him forward to that death in which Christian Baptism finds its foundation and its fulfillment. For this reason Dr. Cullmann appropriately speaks of Jesus' death as his " general baptism." For Jesus, to be baptized means to die. He does not face his cross as a victim caught in the fell clutch of circumstance. He is no tragic hero like Hamlet, who cries:

> " The time is out of joint; — O cursed spite,
>   That ever I was born to set it right! "

He says, instead, " I have a baptism to undergo — what tension I suffer, till it is all over! " " How I am constrained until it is accomplished! " And it is accomplished only when from a cross he cries, " It is finished! " What is finished? The atoning deed, the redemptive act, the victory of God's love.

> " Because he poured out his soul to death,
>   and was numbered with the transgressors;
> yet he bore the sin of many,
>   and made intercession for the transgressors."

" He descended into hell," says the Apostles' Creed — he went through hell for us, for hell is separation, lostness, loneliness, dereliction. " I have a baptism to undergo — what tension I suffer, till it is all over! "

And it is over! It is accomplished in the resurrection power that turns the shadows of the cross into the light of Easter. This is the united testimony of the New Testament and all the centuries of Christian experience. It is finished! A story, whose authenticity we need not here explore, tells how the news of Napoleon's last defeat reached England. A sailing vessel approached the English coast to semaphore the message from the ship to a sentinel on Winchester Cathedral, who in turn signaled it on to the waiting courier. The anxiously awaited message began, " Wellington defeated " — when a dense fog blotted out the rest, and the heartbreaking news went on to London. Then the fog lifted, and the completed message was seen,

" Wellington defeated the enemy " — news the more glorious for the preceding gloom. So Black Friday became Good Friday in the light of the Easter morning. Christ crucified is Christ risen. It is finished! " He has reconciled us . . . to God in one body through the cross."

This is the baptism of blood. As Dr. Cullmann puts it, " Thus the baptismal death of Christ completed once for all on the cross passes over into church Baptism." Christian Baptism is rooted in the once-for-all event which now becomes the event-for-me. In principle we have received Baptism long ago, says Dr. Cullmann. " There the essential act of Baptism was carried out entirely without our co-operation, and even without our faith." We are reminded once again that Christianity begins not with what we do but with what Christ has done for us.

Baptism bears witness that what he has done *for* me he wills to do *in* me. The act of Baptism does not cleanse me; nor does it limit the grace of God to those who have been baptized. But he who was baptized for me and who died for me, into whose name I am baptized — he cleanses me from the guilt and power of sin.

> " Who is this that comes from Edom,
>   in crimsoned garments from Bozrah,
>   he that is glorious in his apparel,
>   marching in the greatness of his strength?
> " It is I, announcing vindication,
>   mighty to save."

The prophetic picture comes to life in the strong Son of God whose baptism was a baptism of blood. " Why is thy apparel red, and thy garments like his that treads in the wine press? " " I have trodden the wine press alone." " I have a baptism to undergo — what tension I suffer, till it is all over! "

And it is over. " One of the soldiers pierced his side with a spear, and at once there came out blood and water. He who saw it has borne witness — his testimony is true, and he knows that he tells the truth — that you also may believe." The sacrament says, " I do believe."

8

THE DOUBLE SIGN

" This is he who came by water and blood, Jesus Christ, not with the water only but with the water and the blood."

I JOHN 5:6

" Jesus Christ came with the double sign of water and blood — the water of His Baptism as Man and the blood of the atonement that He made by His death."

I JOHN 5:6 (PHILLIPS)

CHRISTIAN FAITH depends upon our answer to Jesus' question: " Who do you say that I am? " Faith's earliest answer said simply, " The Christ of God," and the whole New Testament repeats and interprets this confession of faith. The First Letter of John says, " Every one who believes that Jesus is the Christ is a child of God." To know Jesus is to be in God's family.

Jesus' question goes beyond the merely historical question, " Who *was* Jesus? " Who *is* he? What is he to me? If he is only a man who lived several thousand years ago, he cannot concern me ultimately. But if he is the Christ, then God has come to me in him, and to know him is to know God. Not as a stranger, but as one of us God has spoken and come. The man Jesus — the Christ of God! " What therefore God has joined together, let no man put asunder "! So the name declaring what he does becomes part of the name declaring who he is — Jesus Christ.

" Would I suffer for him that I love? So wouldst thou — so wilt
    thou! . . .
    'Tis the weakness in strength, that I cry for! my flesh, that I
    seek
    In the Godhead! I seek and I find it. O Saul, it shall be
    A Face like my face that receives thee; a Man like to me,
    Thou shalt love and be loved by, forever: a Hand like this hand
    Shall throw open the gates of new life to thee! See the Christ
    stand! "

Something disastrous happens when faith forgets this. When
John wrote his letter — as today — many preferred to think of
Christianity as a timeless idea instead of a historic event. After
all, it is a staggering claim to say that in one life actually lived,
in one place and at one time, something has happened that
touches all lives and all places and all times. The philosopher
Lessing objected that the historical can never be of more than
relative importance, that particular facts can never establish
universal truths. We prefer to deal with general truths instead
of insisting upon particular facts. We find it easier to speak of a
" Christ-idea " than to say that Jesus of Nazareth is the Christ
of God.

However, to disassociate the eternal Christ from the man
Jesus makes Christianity a mirage that cannot ultimately help
us because it has not actually happened. Then God would only
have been masquerading as a man without ever making common cause with us, and he would be as far away as ever from a
world of sin and sorrow. Ideas cannot save us — only God can
save. And God can save only as he shares our life to the full.
Precisely here is the miracle and the glory of the Gospel: " The
Word was made flesh, and dwelt among us." The Letter to the
Hebrews puts it: " For the One Who makes men holy and the
men who are made holy share a common humanity. So that He
is not ashamed to call them His brothers " (Phillips).

" Behold the man! " We see the manhood of the master
clearly at the very outset of his career as he was baptized in the
Jordan.

However, this is but half the truth. Richard Gilder may say:

> " If Jesus Christ is a man, —
>   And only a man, — I say
> That of all mankind I cleave to him,
>   And to him will I cleave alway.
>
> " If Jesus Christ is a god, —
>   And the only God, — I swear
> I will follow him through heaven and hell,
>   The earth, the sea, and the air! "

The poet's lines appear to suggest that it makes little difference which way the vote falls, but it makes an immeasurable difference. If Jesus Christ is only a man, his death is one more victory for human hate and sin. If Jesus Christ is only a man, I dare not give him that devotion which belongs only to God.

Christianity not only says, " Behold the man! " Christianity says, " Behold your God! " " Behold, the Lamb of God, who takes away the sin of the world! " Here is the unutterable mystery of divine love — that " God was in Christ reconciling the world to himself." The cross not only shows us what we have done to him; the cross shows us what God has done for us, stooping to shoulder the estrangement and sin we could not bear. This is what atonement means. God was never more Immanuel, never more with us, than in the abyss of our lostness. " Behold, the Lamb of God, who takes away the sin of the world! "

> " I know not how that Calvary's cross
>   A world from sin could free;
> I only know its matchless love
>   Has brought God's love to me."

We come back to the First Letter of John. " Every one who believes that Jesus is the Christ is a child of God." Can we say it more clearly? Yes, says John, for the sacrament says it more clearly. " Jesus Christ came with the double sign of water and blood — the water of His Baptism as Man and the blood of the atonement that He made by His death."

"This is he who came by water." From the day Jesus appeared at the Jordan to be baptized he fulfills all righteousness. He is a man among men. He shares our life to the full in baptism, temptation, struggle, and suffering. His baptism makes it clear that there is no place in our experience outside his experience. "Here where we stand," said the message of Evanston, "Jesus Christ stood with us." That is why he can call us his brothers. "Since therefore the children share in flesh and blood, he himself likewise partook of the same nature. . . . For surely it is not with angels that he is concerned but with the descendants of Abraham." Since we are not angels, no angel can help us. "He did not become an angel; He became a *man*." (Phillips.) "Here where we stand, Jesus Christ stood with us."

Yet "not with the water only," says John. Jesus Christ came with the double sign of water and blood. So Christian Baptism not only says, "Behold the man." It knows that Baptism with water is not enough. "Do you not know," says Paul, "that all of us who have been baptized into Christ Jesus were baptized into his death?" Baptism, says an old catechism, is the sign and seal of "remission of sins by his blood and regeneration by his Spirit." We may not forget that "the blood of Jesus his Son cleanses us from all sin."

"And the Spirit is the witness," John concludes, "because the Spirit is truth. There are three witnesses, the Spirit, the water, and the blood; and these three agree." In other words, Baptism is more than a recognition of what has happened; it recognizes that something is happening. "If any man have not the Spirit of Christ, he is none of his."

It comes to this. The Word of God declares that "every one who believes that Jesus is the Christ is a child of God." Lest the Word be obscured by our own words, the sacramental sign declares anew that Jesus Christ is our Lord, that the church is his new creation "by water and the word," and that

"With his own blood he bought her,
And for her life he died."

9

"WHO SHALL SEPARATE US?"

"With the baptism with which I am baptized, you will be baptized."

MARK 10:39

"Do you not know that all of us who have been baptized into Christ Jesus were baptized into his death?"

ROM. 6:3

HUMAN LOVE always has a tragic overtone. David's moving elegy for Saul and Jonathan includes the familiar line:

> ". . . beloved and lovely!
>   In life and in death they were not divided."

In life and in death! Love yearns for a union beyond this life, and Elizabeth Browning speaks for every lover when she says:

> "I love thee to the depth and breadth and height
>   My soul can reach, . . .
>   . . . I love thee with the breath,
>   Smiles, tears, of all my life! — and, if God choose,
>   I shall but love thee better after death."

But does God choose? Can we be sure? Even the happiest and holiest moment of human troth has in it a foreboding shadow: "Till death us do part." We never quite escape the tragic sense of life. We need a word beyond our words.

There is the word of God. The gospel — in word and sacrament — is good news. Yet it is a strange kind of good news, for it reverses all our values and comes to us as the paradox of God. The word of God is like a two-edged sword, cutting so that it may heal and judging so that it may save. Human love says, " In life and in death." God's love says, " In death and in life." Man says, " Live — then die." God says, " Die — then live."

Nowhere is this word of God more forcibly expressed than in Christian Baptism. Baptism speaks of a new birth — but it begins with a death, for the ground of Baptism is the death of Christ. Baptism declares that nothing can separate us from the love of Christ — but it tells me that to be united with his life I must first be united with his death.

Is this a morbid preoccupation — especially when one thinks of infant Baptism? Or is it rather the good news of God? After all, if all we know is life now, death remains the " undiscovered country," and love can never be sure of enduring communion. But if the strong Son of God has come to make our death his own and if he has risen to make his life our own, how different it all becomes! If he has joined us in death, what can separate us from his life? " Who shall separate us from the love of Christ? " Not death, says the apostle, dismissing that possibility at the very outset. " I am sure that neither death nor life, nor angels, nor principalities, nor things present, nor things to come, nor powers, nor height, nor depth, nor anything else in all creation, will be able to separate us from the love of God in Christ Jesus our Lord."

Jesus' followers were slow to realize this, for they loved him and wanted to be with him always. They were afraid of that road to Jerusalem, because they were afraid they would lose him. They wanted only to sit at his right and at his left in glory. Jesus had to tell them that they did not know what they were asking. " Are you able to drink the cup that I drink, or to be baptized with the baptism with which I am baptized? " They reply quickly, " We are able " — but their reply is pathetic, because all too soon events will prove that they are not able. No, they are not able — nor are we. If our hope lies ultimately in our-

selves, it is sadly misplaced. We muster our best resolves only to
see them falter.

> " Sometimes I'm up, sometimes I'm down,
>   Oh, yes, Lord;
> Sometimes I'm almost to de groun,
>   Oh, yes, Lord."

Am I able? Ask anyone who has tried. Ask Paul. " I can will what
is right, but I cannot do it. . . . Wretched man that I am!
Who will deliver me from this body of death? " Who? " Thanks
be to God through Jesus Christ our Lord! "

This is what Jesus means when he speaks of the cup he must
drink and the baptism he must undergo. He points us — as do
the sacraments — to the utter necessity of his sacrifice. He
knows — as the sacraments know — that only if God's love
meets us at the real point of our need, can life become new. He
knows — as the sacraments know — that only as he bears the
burden of our sin and sorrow, our failure and our fear, can we
ever find his life. This is the baptism he undergoes.

Nonetheless, Christian Baptism is also our response to him,
for salvation is not a mechanical transaction but a profoundly
personal experience. If I say that Christ has been crucified for
me, I must also be crucified with him. Only so does the event of
outward history become the saving event of inward history.
Jesus not only told his followers that he had a baptism to undergo; he also told them that they must be baptized with him.
Paul echoes this when he says, " Do you not know that all of us
who have been baptized into Christ Jesus were baptized into his
death? " What does this mean? " Are we to continue in sin that
grace may abound? " Can I remain what I am and blandly assume that " somebody up there likes me "? " By no means! "
cries Paul. " We were buried therefore with him by baptism into
death, so that as Christ was raised from the dead by the glory
of the Father, we too might walk in newness of life. For if we
have been united with him in a death like his, we shall certainly
be united with him in a resurrection like his. . . . If we have

died with Christ, we believe that we shall also live with him."

In Baptism we are not spectators but participants. Baptism is the seal of what Christ does, and also " our engagement to be the Lord's." We take solemn vows for ourselves and for those entrusted to us. The Presbyterian Catechism of 1729 says that " the needful but much neglected duty of improving our Baptism is to be performed by us all our life long . . . for the mortifying of sin and quickening of grace, and by endeavoring to live by faith." This is to say with Paul, " So you must consider yourselves dead to sin and alive to God in Christ Jesus."

Paul, of course, is using here the language of immersion. He says that we are buried or drowned in baptism so that we may rise to a new life, even as Christ was buried and rose. As Emil Brunner puts it: " This self-willed, self-seeking, self-glorifying I must be drowned. And that is not so ' cheap and easy.' It costs much." That may well lead us to ask if immersion is not a much more powerful psychological effect than sprinkling a few drops of water can ever suggest. Yet, as Donald Baillie reflects, it is well to remember " that a powerful psychological effect at the moment is not what matters, and a reliance on emotion may be as dangerous as a lapse into magical ideas. What matters is not momentary emotion but intention and faith." Just as the Lord's Supper does not depend for its effect on a common cup, so the meaning of Baptism is not dependent on the amount of water.

If Baptism means a costly response, how is it different from any other act of sincere dedication? Simply put, Baptism does not leave me to my own resources. It is costly not for the amount of physical discomfort I may undergo at the moment; it is costly because it cost Jesus Christ his life. It is costly because it means that I will really believe that I belong to him and that I really want him to do in me what he has done for me. It is costly because it means that I really want to be united in his death.

Human love says, " In life and in death." Baptism says rather, " In death and in life," for that is the order of Christian faith. Death is no longer the unknown and tragic reality that can threaten or thwart love's abiding communion. Death cannot separate us from the love of God. " If we have, as it were, shared His death, let us rise and live our new lives with Him "! (Phillips.) In his wonderful *Journal,* John Woolman tells us of a desperate illness he had. In a dream he kept hearing the words: " John Woolman is dead. John Woolman is dead." He was frightened and perplexed until he remembered the words, " I have been crucified with Christ; and yet I live."

This is what matters. " He who loses his life for my sake," says Jesus, " will find it." " If we have, as it were, shared His death, let us rise and live our new lives with Him." Each day we need to be immersed in the divine forgiveness. Each day we must repent and put to death all that would separate us from God. " Baptism itself happens just once," writes Brunner again, " but we must believe constantly anew, for only through faith does Baptism save us." After all, we are not baptized only in the name of the Father and the Son, but also in the name of the Holy Spirit. " Now if any man have not the Spirit of Christ, he is none of his."

When Luther became deeply discouraged or distressed, he would write in large letters, " *Baptizatus sum* " — I have been baptized. " Who shall separate us from the love of Christ? . . . Neither death, nor life, . . . nor anything else in all creation." Thanks be to God.

10

FLOOD TIDE

*" Only Noah was left, and those that were with him in the ark.
And the waters prevailed upon the earth."*

GEN. 7:23-24

*" I cannot help pointing out what a perfect illustration this is of
the way you have been admitted to the safety of the Christian
' ark' by baptism, which means, of course, far more than the
mere washing of a dirty body: it means the ability to face God
with a clear conscience. For there is in every true baptism the
virtue of Christ's rising from the dead."*

I PETER 3:20-21 (PHILLIPS)

THE ANALOGY that Peter draws between Baptism and the
Flood appears absurdly exaggerated, and doubly so where
immersion is not practiced. What remote connection is there
between " the fountains of the deep " of the Flood story and a
few drops of water that touch a tiny baby?

Yet withal, the Flood story retains a strange fascination. When
William Armstrong recently described the sudden death of his
wife he did so in a moving little book called *Through Troubled
Waters*. He writes: " The waters rise almost imperceptibly and
without notice. Around a tree or embankment there is a whirl-
ing, gentle and silent. Sometimes the silence is broken with a
muffled laughterlike sound as the water dances with the thing it
will destroy. Then almost without sound, except a faint gurgling
swallow, the tree or the embankment slips into the flood and

is no more." He portrays the whole gamut of his sorrow in the
imagery of the Flood story — cloud patterns, flood, undertow,
ebbtide, mist, raindrops, and covenant. His is a contemporary
expression of the psalmist's words: " Thou carriest them away
as with a flood."

Water is a strangely powerful symbol. Water creates life —
and destroys it. It nourishes life — and drowns it. Water symbolizes both healing influences and abysmal chaos.

The Bible knows this. If it speaks of the water of life, it also
sees in water primeval chaos and overwhelming woe. " Darkness
was upon the face of the deep." At times the deep threatens to
sweep away all order and all meaning. A man like Jonah cries
out:

> " For thou didst cast me into the deep,
> into the heart of the seas,
> And the flood was round about me;
> all thy waves and thy billows
> passed over me. . . .
> The waters closed in over me,
> the deep was round about me."

Old Testament thought often sees in the bottomless deep the
unknown terrors of chaos and the uncontrollable monsters of
Rahab and Leviathan. When the floodgates of the deep are un-
leashed, what can survive?

Yet the men of the Bible knew that though the waters can
close over them, the waters cannot close over God, for God is
the Creator of the deep and he is Lord over the floods. " The
Spirit of God was moving over the face of the waters."

> " When the waters saw thee, O God,
> when the waters saw thee, they were afraid,
> yea, the deep trembled."

This, the Flood story declares. God remembers Noah and
God brings the ark to safety. At length the waters recede and
the green land appears again as the earth is renewed in resurrection. God sets his bow in the sky and remembers his covenant.

" And God said, ' This is the sign of the covenant which I make
between me and you and every living creature that is with you,
for all future generations. . . . When the bow is in the clouds,
I will look upon it and remember the everlasting covenant."
Thus the story of the Flood is not so much the story of destruc-
tion as it is the story of salvation.

For this reason the First Letter of Peter sees an analogy between the Flood and Baptism. The water of Baptism, like the
water of the Flood, symbolizes for the writer the end of an old
life, for it sweeps an old aeon into oblivion. The old life, as the
old world, must die if a new life and a new world are to be born.
He points out that Baptism means much more than the cleansing judgment of God. The same Spirit who moved over the face
of the deep to create light and life moves over the sign of the
baptismal water. The same God who saved Noah through the
Flood is still calling and gathering his people today. It is not at
all surprising that one of the most loved symbols for the church
— currently the emblem of the World Council of Churches —
is the ark upon the waters. Noah was saved not in spite of the
Flood but through the Flood, and so are God's children still.

> " When through the deep waters I call thee to go,
>   The rivers of woe shall not thee overflow."

Out of the Flood a resurrected world appears. Out of the agony
and death of Golgotha comes a resurrection morning, and a new
world is born. It means that God is never nearer to his world
than in the judgment that saves. That is why Peter can write:
" I cannot help pointing out what a perfect illustration this is of
the way you have been admitted to the safety of the Christian
' ark ' by baptism. . . . For there is in every true baptism the
virtue of Christ's rising from the dead."

Noah did not deserve his salvation — nor do I. But God is
gracious and still remembers his covenant, for he has given himself in pledge. The new covenant is not written in the order of
nature by a bow in the sky. It is written in the order of history
by the blood of a cross. This God eternally sees and remembers.

So the sign of death becomes the sign of life. " For there is in every true baptism the virtue of Christ's rising from the dead." The new world has appeared in Jesus Christ, and the sign of the covenant links each child of God with this resurrection and this life.

As Noah believed the promise and entered the ark, so in Baptism we enter the environment of God's grace with a " humble and a contrite heart." Since God's covenant creates a people, Noah's family is with him. So the sign of Baptism is a covenant promise, " For the promise is unto you, and to your children, and to all that are afar off, even as many as the Lord our God shall call."

Baptism declares that our salvation begins and ends in the love of God. To trust that love, to place ourselves under the sign of his promise, is to enter that frail but believing vessel which is the church — " his new creation by water and the word." And the gates of hell shall not prevail against it.

This is our Christian assurance: we " appeal to God for a clear conscience, through the resurrection of Jesus Christ." The sign of God's love is greater than a bow in the sky. It is a cross on a hill, where all the deep closed over God's dear Son only to be rolled away by the power of his resurrection.

The deep may swirl about me, the floods may rise about my feet and may snatch all else from my grasp, but God's love will not let me go.

" Fear not, for I have redeemed you;
    I have called you by name, you are mine.
When you pass through the waters I will be with you;
    and through the rivers, they shall not overwhelm you."

" For beyond the bounds of space and time," concludes William Armstrong, " but within the bounds of children's certain dreams, the Shepherd stands watch ' beside the still waters.' "

11

IS CHRISTIANITY HARD OR EASY?

" Are not Abana and Pharpar, the rivers of Damascus, better than all the waters of Israel? Could I not wash in them, and be clean? "

II KINGS 5:12

A FEW drops of water, a few words spoken — this simple ritual portrays our entrance into the people of God. Is it all not too easy, too ordinary? Ought the sign of the new life not to demand more of us? The question, of course, points to a larger question. Is Christianity hard or easy?

A half-forgotten page of the Old Testament has a parable for us. Naaman, the Syrian commander, was a great man among men, but he was a leper. No cure had been found to heal him of his dread disease. However, a little Israelite maid was sure that if only he would see the prophet of God, a cure could be found. Naaman listens and, armed with official visas and credentials, he travels to Israel. Yet all the prophet tells him to do is to wash seven times in the Jordan. The Syrian leaves in hot anger and disappointment at this absurd command, for he had expected something very different and demanding. " Are not Abana and Pharpar, the rivers of Damascus, better than all the waters of Israel? Could I not wash in them, and be clean? " His servants remonstrate, saying: " If the prophet had commanded you to do some great thing, would you not have done it? How much rather, then, when he says to you, ' Wash, and be clean '? " Happily, the Syrian was not too proud to listen, and when he had washed in the Jordan, " his flesh was restored like the flesh of a little child, and he was clean."

Let the story be a parable. Where shall I find cleansing from the disease of sin? How can I be restored to wholeness of life when " there is no health in us "? All other remedies have failed. If God is " the health of my countenance," how and where can I find him? And God still speaks his word.

What does God tell me to do? Does he tell me to leave the world of every day for some pilgrimage into a more rarefied atmosphere, far from the dust and toil of the commonplace? Is religion some otherworldly withdrawal from this world? Tennyson's " The Holy Grail " pictures Arthur's knights leaving the tasks of the Round Table, lured by a Holy Grail into a distant and futile quest. At the end Arthur says:

> " And spake I not too truly, O my knights?
>   Was I too dark a prophet when I said
>   To those who went upon the Holy Quest,
>   That most of them would follow wandering fires,
>   Lost in the quagmire? — lost to me and gone,
>   And left me gazing at a barren board,
>   And a lean Order — scarce return'd a tithe —
>   And out of those to whom the vision came
>   My greatest hardly will believe he saw.
>   Another hath beheld it afar off,
>   And, leaving human wrongs to right themselves,
>   Cares but to pass into the silent life.
>   And one hath had the vision face to face,
>   And now his chair desires him here in vain,
>   However they may crown him otherwhere."

Some religions would write off the world of time and sense, but Christianity knows that unless redeeming love can touch the world of every day it cannot touch us anywhere. Jesus prayed for his disciples, " I do not pray that thou shouldst take them out of the world, but that thou shouldst keep them from the evil one."

If not withdrawal, what then? Does God tell me that I must save myself in this world before he will receive me as his child? Would it be too cheap a salvation not to say this? Just here many earnest seekers have not listened to what God has to say. It is all too tempting to turn the gospel of grace into a way of works, a moralism that wants to pile up credits and to earn salvation. A Paul or a Luther had ample occasion to discover the fatal flaw in such endeavor. If *I* am my problem, then all the things I want to do are still vitiated by what I *am*. The more desperately I try to wash my stains, the more my sin remains. Lady Macbeth may wash her stained hands a thousand times, but always it is there — " that damned spot." Alas, all the waters of Abana and Pharpar, all the streams of human goodness, have not been able to cleanse the sin of the soul. " Is there no balm in Gilead? Is there no physician there? "

What does the word of God say? Strangely enough, God tells me that I do not need to do anything, because he has done it for me. He tells me to go to Jordan, to one small and sacred stream of redemptive history. He tells me to come

> " Just as I am, and waiting not
> To rid my soul of one dark blot."

He tells me that he will accept me there.

Is this not too easy? Is it enough to accept the fact that he will accept me? How strange is God's grace! Can this river of grace do what all other streams have failed to do? Can a righteousness of faith accomplish what all my fevered efforts to win righteousness by works cannot do? Is Christianity so easy?

Yes, and paradoxically that is why it is hard. To go to the Jordan means to give up all my pretensions and acknowledge humbly that all my resources are unavailing. That means the end of pride. Is this easy? Is it not rather the stumbling block? " Are not Abana and Pharpar, the rivers of Damascus, better than all the waters of Israel? " Can I really believe that only in that one river of grace God will do what I have not been able to do? Do I really believe this God who says: " I will sprinkle

clean water upon you, and you shall be clean from all your un-
cleannesses, and from all your idols I will cleanse you. A new
heart I will give you, and a new spirit I will put within you "?

Is such salvation hard or easy? It is so easy that a child can
receive it. It is so hard that only a child can receive it. " Except
ye . . . become as little children, ye shall not enter into the
kingdom of heaven."

This is the stumbling block of the gospel. " God chose what
is low and despised in the world, even things that are not, to
bring to nothing things that are, so that no human being might
boast in the presence of God. He is the source of your life in
Christ Jesus, whom God made our wisdom, our righteousness
and sanctification and redemption."

Happy the man who, like Naaman, is not too proud to turn
away from this word of grace. Happy the man who is ready to
give himself to this Lord who says, " Be clean."

What, then, is an adequate portrayal of such salvation?
Should my reception into the community of salvation be dram-
atized by difficult and strenuous rites, by wearisome pilgrim-
ages or burdensome commandments? Must not the sacrament
say what the word of grace says? Can it not be portrayed in utter
simplicity with a few drops of water and a gracious word from
him who says, " I will; be clean "? Does God not still choose
what is low and despised that no human being might boast in
the presence of God?

> " Foul, I to the fountain fly;
>   Wash me, Savior, or I die."

As Naaman's " flesh was restored like the flesh of a little
child," so the water of Baptism reminds us that " whosoever
shall not receive the kingdom of God as a little child shall in
no wise enter therein." There is no other way.

12

DEDICATION IS NOT ENOUGH

" I have baptized you with water; but he will baptize you with the Holy Spirit."

MARK 1:8

" Jesus answered, ' Truly, truly, I say to you, unless one is born of water and the Spirit, he cannot enter the kingdom of God.' "

JOHN 3:5

" ' Did you receive the Holy Spirit when you believed? ' And they said, ' No, we have never even heard that there is a Holy Spirit.' And he said, ' Into what then were you baptized? ' "

ACTS 19:2

THE EARLY CHURCH had to choose between the baptism of John and the Baptism of Jesus. In a very real sense that issue is urgently contemporary. Let us see why.

What is wrong with the church? In a time when men's hunger for God is everywhere apparent and when the church faces an unparalleled opportunity, why is the church not more truly a redemptive community? What is lacking?

These questions troubled Paul as he came to Ephesus. He found there a Christian church strategically located, one that had enjoyed eloquent preaching, a church full of sincere and dedicated people. Yet he saw at once that this church was noticeably lacking in spiritual power. What was wrong?

Paul did not begin with a survey of its organizational structure. Instead, he asked a leading question: " Did you receive the

Holy Spirit when you believed? " A little lady asked a similar question as she was being shown the glories of a great cathedral. She suddenly turned to her guide with a leading question: "Young man, young man, stop your chatter and tell me, has anyone been saved here lately? "

The question, whether asked in Paul's day or in our own, can be disconcerting. It cannot be answered by statistics or programs. In plain fact, it is *the* question that needs answering, yet often the last question asked. " Did you receive the Holy Spirit when you believed? "

Paul's friends said, " No, we have never even heard that there is a Holy Spirit." The answer is honest — and tragic. So that was it! These Christians had been like men trying to row across the sea instead of unfurling a sail so that God's strong wind might fill the sail and drive them forward. The Holy Spirit is not a luxury in Christian life or worship, but a necessity.

> " In vain we tune our formal songs,
>   In vain we strive to rise;
> Hosannas languish on our tongues,
>   And our devotion dies."

The answer? " Come, Holy Spirit."

Paul was perplexed. " Into what then were you baptized? " They answered, " Into John's baptism." Paul replied, " John baptized with the baptism of repentance, telling the people to believe in the one who was to come after him, that is, Jesus." The story has a happy conclusion, for the Ephesian church eagerly turned to Christian Baptism, and " the Holy Spirit came on them."

Why was Paul so concerned about Baptism? If Baptism is the rite of initiation into the Christian community, the meaning we attach to Baptism may well reflect our understanding of Christianity itself. What does your Baptism mean to you?

One suspects that the church of Ephesus has many parallels today — people who are earnest and sincere and dedicated, but for whom God's new day has not yet come. For them Baptism expresses only dedication and yearning, not the seal of God's Holy Spirit. They know the baptism of John but not the Baptism of Jesus.

This is not said to disparage them — or John. It is not said to minimize the importance of repentance and dedication. Jesus hailed John as one of the greatest born of women, but he also said that " he who is least in the kingdom of God is greater than he [John]." John knew that his role was preparatory. " I have baptized you with water; but he will baptize you with the Holy Spirit." John expresses man's need. Jesus answers it. That is why John is not offended when his own followers leave him to follow Jesus. " He must increase, but I must decrease." The baptism of repentance is a prelude and prophecy of the Baptism of the Spirit. Beyond all moralism — the gospel!

It is interesting to observe how Jesus himself deals with the problem. Nicodemus was a sincerely dedicated man, yet Jesus says to him bluntly, " Truly, truly, I say to you, unless one is born anew, he cannot see the kingdom of God." It is not enough for a man to try harder, for salvation is rebirth, not reformation. Nicodemus does not understand. Can Jesus say it more clearly? Yes, he can. " Truly, truly, I say to you, unless one is *born of water and the Spirit*, he cannot enter the kingdom of God."

Christian Baptism says this clearly — water and Spirit. Water is more than the sign of cleansing; it becomes the sign of rebirth. " If any one is in Christ, he is a new creation." This makes Christian Baptism radically different from all the ritual purifications of former religion. The water of Baptism no longer points merely to our need; it points to a new life.

If Nicodemus had difficulty in understanding this, so do we. But Jesus reminds him — and us — that we do not need to fathom the origin of the new life or chart the course of God's Spirit to understand that God makes us new. " The wind blows where it wills, and you hear the sound of it, but you do not know whence it comes or whither it goes; so it is with every one who is born of the Spirit." It is well that we cannot channel or limit the Spirit of God. God is not limited to this sacramental seal, though it is a legitimate expression of his Spirit. We ought not to " quench the Spirit " by speculating about the necessity of Baptism for salvation. Baptism declares that God's Spirit makes men new. It calls us beyond our dedication to his action.

John's baptism still yearns for a Savior to come, but Christian Baptism is grounded in the redemptive deed of Christ. So the conversation with Nicodemus — as indeed every conversation of Christian faith — leads irresistibly to the atoning deed. " No one has ascended into heaven but he who descended from heaven, the Son of man." And this coming of God into life is at infinite cost. " So must the Son of man be lifted up, that whoever believes in him may have eternal life " — and we are pointed to the cross.

The pity is that then and now the meaning of the cross has often been obscured in Christian worship. If Paul was astonished to find that thirty years after Calvary a Christian congregation should see in Baptism — and in faith — only a dedicatory rite that forgot the gift of God, would Paul not be more astonished to find that after twenty centuries the gospel is still mistaken for an impossible summons instead of a gracious deed? If the gifted preacher of Ephesus, Apollos, distorted the gospel despite all his eloquent zeal, is many a gifted preacher not doing so still? If Paul had to remind the church of his day that men are saved by faith in God, not by faith in their own faith, does not our age need this reminder? The church becomes the community of salvation not through programs but through a Person, not through ecclesiastical structures but through God's Spirit. " Not by might, nor by power, but by my Spirit, says the Lord of hosts."

The early church recognized the issue. The church of today needs to do so. Our worship in sacrament always expresses our understanding of faith. " On hearing this, they were baptized in the name of the Lord Jesus. And . . . the Holy Spirit came on them."

" Gracious Spirit, dwell with me;
I myself would gracious be;
And with words that help and heal
Would thy life in mine reveal;
And with actions bold and meek
Would for Christ my Savior speak."

LIFE IN HIS SPIRIT

" Help me in this high endeavor,
  Father, Son, and Holy Ghost!
Bind my heart to thee for ever,
  Till I join the heavenly host."

13

RETURN AND RENEWAL

*" He went away again across the Jordan to the place where John
at first baptized, and there he remained."*

JOHN 10:40

THIS INTERLUDE in the life of Jesus comes between the grow-
ing hostility of Jerusalem and the final days that lead to the
cross. " He went away again across the Jordan to the place where
John at first baptized, and there he remained."

Why did he go there? Was Jesus seeking a temporary in-
cognito to avoid the crowds? All the Gospels indicate that the
closer he came to the cross the more he withdrew from the
crowds. Was it to avoid a premature arrest? The Fourth Gospel
has just indicated that the authorities had tried to arrest him
but that he had escaped from their hands, for his hour had not
yet come.

There is a stronger reason. Amid the conflicting voices of his
friends and his foes Jesus must hear the voice of God. Let no
one suppose that he was not troubled by the same anxieties that
beset us all. He " was in all points tempted like as we are." The
Synoptic Gospels express this in the anxious wrestling of Geth-
semane. This Gospel does not describe the agony of Gethsem-
ane, yet in its own way it bears witness to the humanity of the
Savior. How shall Jesus recognize God's will in the midst of the
conflicting wills of friend and foe? How? " He went away again
across the Jordan to the place where John at first baptized, and
there he remained."

Why there? Because there at the beginning of his ministry Jesus had been baptized. There he had seen the heavens opened and had heard so clearly the voice of God: " Thou art my beloved Son; with thee I am well pleased." There Jesus had heard God's call — a call that told him the road of Messiahship was the road of the Suffering Servant who " was numbered with the transgressors." Now, as that road is about to reach its dread conclusion, Jesus returns to the place of first certainty so that the Voice he had heard before may speak clearly again to rule out all false choices and to direct him unwaveringly to his appointed task. In Donald Miller's words, a " homing sense of the spirit of Jesus" drove him back to the place of beginnings. " And there he remained " — until he was renewed in spirit and ready for the great encounter.

If Jesus needed such return and renewal, is it otherwise with us? Is it not much more true of us? Are we not constantly beset with conflicting choices? Are we not so often enmeshed in the anxieties of the moment that we cannot read the signposts of the road ahead or adequately discern our life's meaning?

Let no one suppose that a man of faith is immune to such bewildering uncertainty. Listen to the psalmist:

" I cry aloud to God,
    aloud to God, that he may hear me.
  In the day of my trouble I seek the Lord;
  in the night my hand is stretched out without wearying;
    my soul refuses to be comforted.
  I think of God, and I moan;
    I meditate, and my spirit faints."

How can I be sure, he asks? How do I know that God will hear me? " Has God forgotten to be gracious? " The psalmist knows that he must go back beyond his own fluctuating experience of God if he is to find assurance.

" I will call to mind the deeds of the Lord;
        yea, I will remember thy wonders of old."

In the clarity of God's redemptive power in history, he finds his own clarity and conviction renewed.

Can I call to mind some blessed deed of God? Can I go back to a place of utter certainty? There is a creative power in memory, as everyone knows. Significantly, the men of the Bible are constantly going back to a place of bedrock certainty. After a nearly fatal detour in Egypt, Abraham goes back to Bethel, " to the place where his tent had been at the beginning." We see Moses leading his people to the mount where God had first spoken to him. And in a day when nothing seemed sure and when his own faith faltered, Elijah returns to that same mount, where he hears the selfsame voice of God.

Where shall I go? Shall I go back to some place in my own experience when I was sure and when I stood firm? Let us grant that many a Christian loves to recall some " happy day that fixed my choice." Such memory has its strength — but it also has its danger. It might lead to a sad nostalgia as I try to re-create some subjective mood of long ago.

> " What peaceful hours I once enjoyed!
> How sweet their memory still!
> But they have left an aching void
> The world can never fill."

Is it enough to try to return to some past feeling of my own? The psalmist did not find it so.

Is it not better to go back to some place of stronger certainty? " I will call to mind the deeds of the Lord." I need a stronger voice and a stronger deed than any I have mustered in times past. Is there some place where redemptive history has touched my life in unmistakable fashion?

Jesus found himself going back to the place of his baptism. Is there a better place to go? Baptism is not primarily the place where I declared for God. Indeed, for most of us it happened in infancy, long before we were conscious of any feelings of our own. Rather, Baptism declared once and forever that God has laid his hand on me. Baptism declared that long before I ever sought the Lord of grace and glory, he sought me and claimed me for himself. Baptism declared that he who gave himself in sacrificial love did so *for me*. Baptism declared that the God of Jesus Christ is *my* God — not because I loved him but because he loved me. Baptism says that " when the goodness and loving kindness of God our Savior appeared, he saved us, not because of deeds done by us in righteousness, but in virtue of his own mercy, by the washing of regeneration and renewal in the Holy Spirit, which he poured out upon us richly through Jesus Christ our Savior, so that we might be justified by his grace and become heirs in hope of eternal life. The saying is sure."

Yes, it is sure. That is why Luther could find assurance in his discouragement by saying, " *Baptizatus sum* " (I have been baptized).

> " Blessed Savior, who hast taught me
>   I should live to thee alone,
> All these years thy hand hath brought me,
>   Since I first was made thine own.
> At the font my vows were spoken
>   By my parents in the Lord:
> That my vows shall be unbroken,
>   At the altar I record."

To go back to the place of Baptism for renewal is to rediscover the steadying certainty that we love him because he first loved us. To go back to the place of beginnings is to learn afresh that " God's firm foundation stands, bearing this seal: 'The Lord knows those who are his.' "

Such return is no escape from present duty. It offers no false confidence and makes no false guarantees. But it clears my vision, it nerves my energies, it quickens my devotion to him who has begun a good work in me and will bring it to completion.

The road into tomorrow comes out of yesterday. In that wartime novel *Mrs. Miniver*, the author pictures an annual family trip to Scotland, this time full of memories as the war clouds gather. After stopping awhile to rest and relax, " Mrs. Miniver let the clutch in and set off on the long descent to Appleby. In the convex driving-mirror she could see, dwindling rapidly, the patch of road where they had stood; and she wondered why it had never occurred to her before that you cannot successfully navigate the future unless you keep always framed beside it a small clear image of the past."

What patch of hallowed ground can help to chart and guide my course? Jesus said, "Learn of me." "He went away again across the Jordan to the place where John at first baptized, and there he remained."

14

END AND BEGINNING

*" It is done! I am the Alpha and the Omega, the beginning and
the end."*

Rev. 21:6

In his Christmas oratorio, " For the Time Being," W. H. Auden reflects:

> " To those who have seen
> The Child, however dimly, however incredulously,
> The Time Being is, in a sense, the most trying time of all."

He pictures the three Wise Men who represent men's yearning
for life's meaning and purpose. From varying quests they all
unite to say:

> " To discover how to be human now
> Is the reason we follow the star."

On the other hand, the three shepherds have been so preoccupied with the present moment that they have never really begun to think about ultimate meaning. One of them says:

> " The winter night requires our constant attention,
> Watching that water and good will,
> Warmth and well-being, may still be here in the morning."

Yet there must be more, and another says:

> " What is real
> About us all is that each of us is waiting."

There you have it. Whether in seeking or in waiting, the present time cries out for meaning, for life must have some ultimate significance.

> "We who must die demand a miracle.
>   How could the Eternal do a temporal act,
>   The Infinite become a finite fact?
>   Nothing can save us that is possible:
>   We who must die demand a miracle."

The miracle happens, for Christ is born, and Wise Men and shepherds come to the manger. The Wise Men know that their quest has found its goal, so they greet the Child with the words:

> "O here and now our endless journey stops."

The shepherds know that life now can never content itself with what it has been, so they salute the Child with the words:

> "O here and now our endless journey starts."

This is forever the paradox of Advent — the coming of the glory of the Lord. One of the Advent hymns sings:

> "Yea, through life, death, through sorrow and through sinning
>   He shall suffice me, for he hath sufficed;
> Christ is the end, for Christ was the beginning,
>   Christ the beginning, for the end is Christ."

All this is simply to recognize the voice of Him who says, " It is done! I am the Alpha and the Omega, the beginning and the end."

Christian Baptism also hears this voice. As P. T. Forsyth wrote: " New Testament Baptism was a relative goal, a crisis, a committal crowning the preparation of the Word. . . . And it was also a point of departure for the new life, an era to date from, an occasion central and fontal for the life in Christ and his community. . . . It ended the way *to* Christ, and began the life *in* Christ." Baptism, like Advent, marks an end and a beginning.

If we forget that Baptism marks the end of the way to Christ, it becomes but one more expression of our yearning for God, one more milestone in the never-ending and never-realized quest for life's meaning and salvation. But Baptism, like Advent, has a gracious word. It declares that we need not look farther for life's meaning for God's grace. It proclaims that God's grace and glory have come to us in Jesus Christ. It declares that the miracle has happened — the Infinite has become a finite fact for us! Baptism says what the Word of the cross says: " It is finished." Baptism says what the risen Lord says: " It is done!" Therefore we can and must say, " O here and now our endless journey stops."

Let us take this to heart. Time and again Augustine's mother postponed her son's Baptism, even when he was critically ill. Monica was afraid that sin after Baptism might jeopardize his soul's welfare. Her misguided concern forgot the word of Him who says, " It is done! "

The Evanston Assembly recognized this relation between having and hoping. " Our hope is not the projection of our desires upon an unknown future, but the product in us of God's acts in history, and above all of his act in raising Jesus Christ from the dead." Paul constantly thrills to the fact of the finished deed. " He has delivered us from the dominion of darkness and transferred us to the kingdom of his beloved Son, in whom we have redemption, the forgiveness of sins." This, Christ has done, says the apostle. " Christ has utterly wiped out the damning evidence of broken laws and commandments which always hung over our heads, and has completely annulled it by nailing it over His own Head on the Cross. And then, having drawn the sting of all the powers ranged against us, He exposed them, shattered, empty and defeated, in His final glorious triumphant act "! (Phillips.)

If the Lord of Baptism says, " It is done," shall we hinder or delay the sign of his victory within the community of faith? Baptism, like Advent, proclaims the end of an old world and the birth of a new. Why should we seek other light than the light that has shone in Jesus Christ our Lord? " O here and now our endless journey stops."

However, let us not lose the paradox. If Baptism ends the way *to* Christ, it begins the life *in* Christ. " O here and now our endless journey starts."

Not to say this would make Baptism magical and faith complacent. We have seen how emphatically Paul can speak about the finished character of redemption. Yet he also insists that " this reconciliation assumes, of course, that you maintain a firm position in the faith, and do not allow yourselves to be shifted away from the hope of the Gospel" (Phillips). Elsewhere he illustrates by analogy. " I want you to know, brethren, that our fathers were all under the cloud, and all passed through the sea, and all were baptized into Moses in the cloud and in the sea, and all ate the same supernatural food and all drank the same supernatural drink." The redemptive deed was done in that never-to-be-forgotten exodus from Egypt. " Nevertheless with most of them God was not pleased; for they were overthrown in the wilderness." Let this warn us, he cautions, for these things " were written down for our instruction, upon whom the end of the ages has come. Therefore let any one who thinks that he stands take heed lest he fall."

Both Roman Catholic and Protestant Christians misunderstand Baptism when this is obscured. When the Roman Catholic speaks of an " infused grace " through Baptism, the gift becomes an impersonal substance instead of the declaration of a personal relationship with Christ. When the Protestant separates Baptism from the whole life of faith he makes it an empty rite. " We may not give Baptism," says Forsyth, " unless we also bring the gospel and promise to keep bringing it, to the young life till it can assume responsibility in confirmation or in taking up membership."

It is not different in adult Baptism. Initiation into the body of Christ is not the end of faith but rather its beginning. No one can be content with what he is, no matter how compelling his conversion may have been. No one can say that he " has ar-

rived." We cannot be content, says Paul, " until we all attain
to the unity of the faith and of the knowledge of the Son of
God, to mature manhood, to the measure of the stature of the
fullness of Christ."

How long will that take? Is even a lifetime sufficient? Listen
to Moses at the end of his life: " O Lord God, thou hast only
begun to show thy servant thy greatness and thy mighty hand."
A hundred and twenty years old — and he says that he is only
beginning to see! Listen to Paul, whose life has for years been
a glorious comradeship with Christ: " Not that I have already
obtained this or am already perfect; but I press on to make it
my own, because Christ Jesus has made me his own." Paul's
quest for salvation had ended the day he met his Lord, but, in
deeper sense, his journey began that day on the Damascus road.

Christ is the End and the Beginning. In Auden's words, " The
Time Being is, in a sense, the most trying time of all," for it
rules out all complacency. But it is a glorious time, for it is the
time of Advent for the soul, the time of Christ. The Lord of this
time — and of all time — says: " It is done! I am the Alpha and
the Omega, the beginning and the end."

If he says, " It is done! " — I can say, " Thy will be done "!

15

MODE OR MEANING

" Simon Peter said to him, ' Lord, not my feet only but also my hands and my head!' Jesus said to him, ' He who has bathed does not need to wash, except for his feet, but he is clean all over.' "

JOHN 13:9-10

MUCH CONTROVERSY has centered on the proper mode of Baptism — sprinkling, pouring, immersion. We may grant that each mode has its own particular psychological effect — but does the meaning of Baptism depend upon its psychological impact? The pity is that very often questions about the mode of Baptism have crowded out the more important question of its meaning. Here a familiar story from the Fourth Gospel can help us.

John is the only Evangelist who describes Jesus washing his disciples' feet. What does he see in this incident?

Some say it is solely an object lesson in humility. Certainly it is that. Luke tells us that the disciples were quarreling at the Supper about greatness while Jesus said, " I am among you as one who serves." In that setting the story of the foot washing has reason enough. " Jesus, knowing that the Father had given all things into his hands, and that he had come from God and was going to God, rose from supper, laid aside his garments, and girded himself with a towel." Here is real greatness! How much the disciples have to learn from their master! " I have

given you an example, that you also should do as I have done
to you."

Others believe that Jesus intended the act as a permanent
rite. Because he said, " You also ought to wash one another's
feet," certain modern churches continue this practice as an act
of worship.

Still others believe that the story points to Christian Baptism.
Dr. Cullmann points out that the Fourth Evangelist constantly
links together the sacraments of Baptism and the Supper and
sees both as deriving from the riven side of the crucified Lord.
Now, as the hour of the crucifixion is at hand, the water and
the blood are joined once more, for the water precedes the cup
as Baptism precedes reception to the Supper in worship. If one
objects that the story does not speak explicitly of Baptism, Cullmann would remind us that John does not directly speak of the
Supper either, though he constantly portrays the life of Jesus
in sacramental language. " What I am doing you do not know
now, but afterward you will understand."

Be that as it may, the story of the foot washing can offer some
helpful perspectives concerning Baptism, for the questions that
Peter raises are also questions raised by the sacrament.

When Jesus began to wash their feet, Peter objected, " You
shall never wash my feet." Peter is not defiant. He is no Henley
who wants to be the master of his fate. Peter is a Christian who
has sincerely confessed Christ as the master of his fate. Yet
Peter, as many of us, is still offended by the way of the cross. He
wants to serve, to endure, to dare. Well and good — but he is
really more sure of himself than he is sure of Christ. " I will lay
down my life for you." The trouble is that as long as he is sure
of himself he does not see the necessity of the cross. How hard
it is to learn that Christian faith does not begin with what I do
or can ever do — but with what Christ is and does! The more
zealous the disciple, the harder the lesson.

This applies to our approach to the sacraments also. It is very
easy to make of the sacraments *my* expression of loyalty, *my*
dedication, *my* faith. " How very hard it is to be a Christian,"

said Christina Rossetti. How very hard — even in Baptism!

Jesus replies to his well-meaning disciple, " If I do not wash you, you have no part in me." Peter's zeal needs cleansing as much as Peter's cowardice will need forgiveness. All my resolves, all my intentions, all my efforts need cleansing.

> " Not the labors of my hands
> Can fulfill thy law's demands."

Baptism also says, " Thou must save, and thou alone." That is why Baptism is primarily his act, not mine.

" Lord," Peter says, " not my feet only but also my hands and my head! " One cannot help liking Peter for his enthusiasm and for his readiness to repent. Is his request not laudable? Isn't he saying what Christian piety always wants to say?

> " Whiter than snow, Lord,
> Wash me just now,
> As in thy presence
> Humbly I bow."

Why then does Jesus answer, " He who has bathed does not need to wash, except for his feet, but he is clean all over "? Would the experience not be more psychologically compelling if Peter had had his wish?

The same might be said of Christian Baptism. Would immersion not be a more compelling experience than sprinkling a few drops of water? Must we not say that some of the New Testament imagery of Baptism, such as Paul's figure of dying and rising, finds more adequate expression in immersion? Doubtless.

Nonetheless, Jesus' word is a needed reminder that our cleansing depends on one thing only — a living relationship with himself. Too much concern with the mode of Baptism can detract rather than enforce its meaning. " Jesus did not mean us to believe in water but in himself," said Schlatter. Nor must we measure the worth of Baptism by the way we feel about it.

" You are clean," the Savior says. We are clean not through

the sacrament but through Him who gives both word and sacrament. We are God's beloved, " called to be saints." " He who calls you is faithful, and he will do it."

" You are clean, *but not all of you.*" The story closes with a severe warning. Judas was washed with water but he was not clean, for he did not want the kind of Savior Jesus proved to be. He refused to listen to his word, and he left the company of Christ and the community of faith. " So, after receiving the morsel, he immediately went out; and it was night." It is always night when one leaves the light of the world.

Do not make Judas a monster of evil. He is a man. " Let any one who thinks that he stands take heed lest he fall." The tragedy of Judas reminds us that our salvation is not in water but in Christ.

All this is not to disparage questions of church order, including baptismal order. Such questions need to be asked and answered as seriously as our understanding of the Scriptures and of our tradition allows us to answer them. Let us be sure only that questions of administration do not take the place of the question of meaning, for the meaning of Baptism is not found in the manner of administration. It is found only in God who " saved us, not because of deeds done by us in righteousness, but in virtue of his own mercy, by the washing of regeneration and renewal in the Holy Spirit, which he poured out upon us richly through Jesus Christ our Savior."

" You were washed, you were sanctified, you were justified in the name of the Lord Jesus Christ and in the Spirit of our God." Are we? That — and that alone — matters.

16

RECLAIMING OUR HERITAGE

*" And Isaac dug again the wells of water which had been dug
in the days of Abraham his father; for the Philistines had
stopped them after the death of Abraham, and he gave them
the names which his father had given them."*

GEN. 26:18

"With joy you will draw water from the wells of salvation."

ISA. 12:3

WHEN we read the patriarchal stories of Genesis, Isaac
appears rather pale and commonplace beside Abraham
and Jacob, for there is nothing spectacular or novel about him.
Yet " the Lord blessed him." Why? Isaac had a lively sense of
heritage. Returning to the heritage of his father, he reclaimed
those wells which had too long been idled and forgotten. From
the wells of the past new life comes to the present.

The story is timely. Too often the church has lost the living
springs of its faith — sometimes by forgetting its heritage in its
quest for new landmarks, sometimes by camping beside the old
landmarks while the springs lie buried and unused despite ancient creeds and honored forms.

What has happened to the wells of salvation? Abraham had
dug deeply into the promises of God. He is remembered as the
father of the faithful because he gave himself in utter trust to
the promises of God. "Abraham believed God," says Paul,
" and it was reckoned to him as righteousness."

What has happened to the wells of salvation? We read that Abraham's wells were rendered useless by Philistine mischief. Who are the Philistines? Questions of historical chronology need not detain us, for the Philistines do not belong merely to the past. Matthew Arnold applied the name " Philistine" to the callous greed and the shallow spirit of late nineteenth-century industrialism that he saw threatening the moral and spiritual climate of his beloved England. Must we not say the same? The deeper springs of our spiritual life have been filled by the tawdry illusions of the secular spirit — the technical skill but the moral poverty of our sensate culture. Says T. S. Eliot:

> " Where is the Life we have lost in living?
> Where is the wisdom we have lost in knowledge?
> Where is the knowledge we have lost in information?
> The cycles of Heaven in twenty centuries
> Bring us farther from God and nearer to the Dust."

A thousand billboards proclaim the Philistine spirit, and this spirit has left its marks on popular religion. What kind of religion is it that croons, " Somebody up there likes me," no matter what I am or what I do? Would not a Jeremiah cry again:

> " Well may the heavens be appalled and shudder;
> for my people have done double wrong,
> they have forsaken me, the reservoir of fresh water,
> and hewn out cisterns for themselves,
> leaky cisterns that cannot hold any water! " (Moffatt)

Contemporary Protestantism does not need new programs so much as it needs a " deeper plunge into the gospel."

The springs of grace are not gone; they need only be rediscovered. The children of Abraham can yet do what Isaac did. Today once again they can dig the wells of living water so that the heritage of the past becomes relevant today and a promise for tomorrow.

" And Isaac dug again the wells of water which had been dug in the days of Abraham his father." It is happening. Ecumenical

Christianity has come into being not by diluting the central issues of faith or by minimizing the traditions of the past but by serious concern about faith and order. Christian unity will come not by scorning creedal landmarks of yesterday but by digging afresh the wells of salvation. " The purpose of the ecumenical movement," as H. T. Kerr reminds us, " is not only to present a united Christian front, but to proclaim a united Christian message. And unless there *is* a united message, any organizational unity will be nothing more than a scaffolding, a façade, literally a ' front.' "

Accordingly, we can be grateful for a rekindled concern with the Bible, with Christian doctrine, and with Christian worship. In the rejuvenated curricula of many Sunday church schools, in communicant preparation for church membership, in summer conferences and lay leadership schools, there are heartening signs that this is not confined to the professional theologians. Christians are exploring again the long-hidden wells of the spirit, for our time has shown us all too plainly the tragic flaws of a Philistine culture. We must have God — the living God.

Since our worship in sacrament is always a rather faithful index of our understanding of Christian faith, it is not at all surprising that our day is manifesting a fresh sacramental concern. Especially is this true of Christian Baptism.

It needs no argument to indicate the central place of Baptism in the worship of the early Christian church. It needs no argument to indicate how far this well has been filled and idled in the years just behind us. As long ago as 1917 Forsyth was complaining: "This is only one of several current indications how the cult of the child in the church may destroy the worship of the gospel; how natural religion drives out the spiritual, and especially evangelical. I have been at many Sunday school anniversaries, and I have found the same thing shown; when all the singing, even of the morning service, was on these occasions given up to children's, not to say babies', hymns, with music to correspond, while Baptism was of little moment, or was hidden away in the home. It is so easy to let a precious rite die, and it is so hard to restore it. It is dropped through misconception or indifference, and it can only be restored by something so hard as the revival of principle, something like a Reformation or a Revolution, the renewal of conviction and the return of earnestness not in one or a few but in a whole community."

But renewal of conviction is taking place. In the fresh explorations of Biblical study, in denominational efforts like that of the Church of Scotland, and in the fresh distillations of the World Council's Faith and Order groups, as in the revival of liturgical concern, the old wells are being dug again and the living water is beginning to flow.

> " Nearer, my God, to thee,
>   Nearer to thee!
> Through Word and sacrament
>   Thou com'st to me."

The well of Baptism is not an end in itself, but the grace of Baptism is the grace of our Lord Jesus Christ. The water of Baptism points us to that living water which breaks forth wherever and whenever Jesus Christ is found. " The water that I shall give . . . ," said Jesus, " will become in him a spring of water welling up to eternal life." He says again, " He who believes in me, as the scripture has said, ' Out of his heart shall flow rivers of living water.' "

> " Spring thou up within my heart,
>   Rise to all eternity."

" With joy you will draw water from the wells of salvation."

17

THE RIVER OF GRACE

" Then he brought me back to the door of the temple; and behold, water was issuing from below the threshold of the temple."

EZEK. 47:1

THIS magnificent vision came to an exile whose nation had been scattered, whose homeland was desolate, and whose Temple had been destroyed. While in Babylonian captivity Ezekiel saw the heavens open and caught a vision of God's new day.

In vision he is transported to Judea, where he sees the City of God and the Temple of the future. He sees a stream of water issuing from the threshold of the Temple. An angel guide measures a thousand cubits and leads him through the water which is ankle deep. A thousand cubits farther, the water rises to his knees, and then to his loins. Finally the river is " deep enough to swim in, a river that could not be passed through." The mystic river carries everything with it, for everywhere it goes, life blossoms and the desert of Arabah becomes like the garden of the Lord. Alongside the river are trees whose leaves of healing do not wither — all " because the water for them flows from the sanctuary." Even stagnant waters become fresh as they are touched by the onward course of the river of grace.

Only a dream? Do not dismiss the vision lightly. Pity the man who cannot dream, for " where there is no vision, the people perish." Men build their earth according to their dreams. When

the prophet Joel sought to describe the Day of the Lord he pictured it as a day of dreams:

> " And it shall come to pass afterward,
>> that I will pour out my spirit on all flesh;
> your sons and your daughters shall prophesy,
>> your old men shall dream dreams,
>> and your young men shall see visions."

When the Christian church was born at Pentecost, Peter recalls
these words and declares that they are fulfilled. A vision of faith
is not stargazing; it becomes actualized in the life of faith.

If Ezekiel's vision seems unreal or unattainable, let God speak
to us in more tangible sign and symbol. What can we see in
Baptism? The water of Baptism is no mirage, for it issues from
historical reality, it flows into present experience, and it is a
foretaste of ultimate fulfillment. The course of the river of grace
is also the course of the sacrament of grace.

In the first place, the prophet sees an ideal temple. So is the
church of Christ his " new creation by water and the word." If
the perfect temple had never been fully realized on earth,
neither has the church ever found adequate and final expression
in the churches. But it is there. " I believe in . . . the holy
catholic church; the communion of saints." The living church
is always imperfectly seen in the churches, yet it always appears
despite their imperfections — the church of the living God, the
pillar and bulwark of the truth.

> " Unshaken as eternal hills,
>> Immovable she stands,
> A mountain that shall fill the earth,
>> A house not made by hands."

Again, as the prophet saw waters issuing from the Temple
threshold, the church too is the font of a sacred stream. No
Protestant will ever make the church the master of the word and
the sacraments, " for one is your Master, even Christ." However, every Protestant must recognize that word and sacrament
are not purely private concerns but are given to the church and

are acts of worship in the church. It is especially important that the water of Baptism be seen as issuing from the threshold of the Temple. We are untrue to New Testament Baptism if we make of the sacrament a private ritual instead of an act of the worshiping congregation. Home "christenings" and private baptisms are contradictions in terms, for the worshiping congregation is quite as immediately concerned as the child or the parent. This is not to say that in times of emergency the church may and should not come to the home or hospital. It does say that Baptism loses all meaning when it is disassociated from the believing community of faith. Of course the Spirit of God is not limited to this or to any stream. Nonetheless, the normal working of the Spirit is in and through the witness and worship of the church. The river of grace still issues from the Temple threshold.

The prophet can see various stages in the river's rise — first to his ankles, then to his knees, soon to his loins, and finally it is too deep to ford. Yet it is the selfsame stream that flows from the sanctuary of God.

As the full depth of the river is not immediately recognized, neither is the full import of God's grace in Baptism. We may be glad this is so, for the various stages in the river's rise correspond to the various stages of our life. God's grace does not destroy Christian growth and nurture, for God deals with us as persons, not puppets. A Christian child can early know the love of God without yet realizing or plumbing the depths of the gospel. As the child grows, his faith deepens and the river of grace assumes more depth. As he reaches confirmation the river becomes a stream to ford. The farther he goes in the Christian life the more he begins to realize the height and depth and length and breadth of the love of God.

> " Dependent on thy bounteous breath,
>   We seek thy grace alone
> In childhood, manhood, age, and death,
>   To keep us still thine own."

Must we not say the same of the baptismal stream? Is it necessary — or even desirable — that a person experience the water
of Baptism at only one level? Must a child be outside the
church? Does not Baptism rather say that from earliest infancy
I am brought into the environment of grace and receive the seal
of God's love? Of course an infant does not feel any effect. But
who is to say how soon a child becomes aware of love — and
why not divine love?

> " I was made a Christian
>   When my name was given,
> One of God's dear children
>   And an heir of heaven.
> In the name of Christian
>   I will glory now,
> Evermore remember
>   My baptismal vow."

Always the river of grace widens and deepens and carries us
along in the limitless expanse of divine love.

> " More deep than the seas is that river,
>   More full than the manifold tides,
> Where forever and ever and ever
>   It flows and abides."

Even at the end of life the Christian knows that he has only
begun to sound its depths.

> " The streams on earth I've tasted
> More deep I'll taste above,
> There to an ocean fullness
> His mercy doth expand,
> And glory, glory dwelleth
> In Immanuel's land."

One thing more. In the prophetic vision, everywhere the river
goes, barren and stagnant regions are transformed into the gar-

den of God. Dr. John Mackay has given frequent expression to this phase of Christian life which is portrayed by the peace of the river that is fulfilled in action. He reminds us of Lanier's "Song of the Chattahoochee," which pictures the Georgian stream that rises in the hills of Habersham and flows through the valleys of Hall. Rushes and laurel and grass would entice the stream to stay:

> "But oh, not the hills of Habersham,
>   And oh, not the valleys of Hall
> Avail: I am fain for to water the plain.
> Downward the voices of Duty call —
> Downward, to toil and be mixed with the main,
> The dry fields burn, and the mills are to turn,
> And a myriad flowers mortally yearn,
> And the lordly main from beyond the plain
>   Calls o'er the hills of Habersham,
>   Calls through the valleys of Hall."

It is so with Christian Baptism. Jesus gave Baptism as part of a great missionary command: "Go therefore and make disciples of all nations, baptizing them." The water he gives is living water which cannot be selfishly contained but must ever spring up to everlasting life. The world waits for the water that flows from the sanctuary, and we may not halt its course.

> "Blest river of salvation,
>   Pursue thy onward way;
> Flow thou to every nation,
>   Nor in thy richness stay."

Does the dream have any basis in reality? Christian hope is always based on having — for we have Jesus Christ. We see not yet all things — but we see Jesus. The stream that flows from the Temple flowed first from the temple of his body. The grace of God portrayed in the baptismal water is no abstraction, for it is the grace of our Lord and Savior Jesus Christ.

Where Christ is, there is his church — and there flows the stream of his transforming grace.

> " Who can faint, while such a river
> Ever flows their thirst to assuage;
> Grace, which, like the Lord the giver,
> Never fails from age to age? "

18

"FORBID THEM NOT"

"See, here is water! What is to prevent my being baptized?"

THE MARRIAGE CEREMONY has a solemn pause where the question is asked: " If there be any here present who knows any just cause why they may not lawfully be joined in marriage, I require him now to make it known, or ever after to hold his peace." The question is not asked that some protesting voice may dramatically speak from the balcony as in *Jane Eyre*. It is asked so that the couple and the congregation may always remember that this troth is made before God, " the Searcher of all hearts."

There is some reason to believe that in the worship of the early church the baptismal formula included a similar question. The story of Philip and the Ethiopian eunuch is especially interesting for its description of the way a convert was initiated into the church. Although the Revised Standard Version rightly indicates that one verse of the narrative is not in all the manuscripts, it is nonetheless needed to make sense of the stranger's question. " And as they went along the road they came to some water, and the eunuch said, ' See, here is water! What is to prevent my being baptized? ' And Philip said, ' If you believe with all your heart, you may.' And he replied, ' I believe that Jesus Christ is the Son of God.' " So the stranger was baptized and goes on his way rejoicing.

Dr. Cullmann suggests with good reason that the question and answer appear to reflect an early liturgical formula which appears elsewhere as well. When Peter sees the Spirit's presence in the household of Cornelius he asks, " Can any one forbid water for baptizing these people who have received the Holy Spirit just as we have? " What hinders Baptism? Here it is almost as if Peter is asking the question of the water. Did not Jesus once say that there are times when God is so evidently present that, should men be silent, the very stones would cry out?

Later, when Peter justifies his mission to the Gentiles before the church of Jerusalem, he tells how his own reluctance was overcome by the course of events. " I remembered the word of the Lord, how he said, ' John baptized with water, but you shall be baptized with the Holy Spirit.' If then God gave the same gift to them as he gave to us when we believed in the Lord Jesus Christ, who was I that I could withstand God? " Shall Peter hinder God's will? Once Jesus had said to Peter, " Get behind me, Satan! You are a hindrance to me." That must not happen again. Man may not forbid what God ordains. Wherever the gospel of Christ is accompanied by the Holy Spirit in response and faith, there the condition of Baptism is fulfilled.

That old liturgical question, " What prevents Baptism? " is still implicitly asked. It still gives us solemn pause. The only valid reason for refusing Baptism is that the condition of Christian discipleship is denied — faith in Christ as Lord and Savior. Where and when the Ethiopian stranger's reply is made, there and then a stranger is a stranger no more but a member of the household of faith. What is to prevent Baptism — what indeed? " Who shall separate us from the love of Christ? "

Unhappily, other reasons have often intruded to hinder Baptism. Not seldom, for example, concern for church order has led Christians to suspect the validity of another's order. " Teacher," said John once to Jesus, " we saw a man casting out demons in your name, and we forbade him, because he was not following us." But John had no right to forbid — " Do not forbid him." Is it not a tragic irony that Methodism became a separate communion because John Wesley's right to ordain was questioned by the church of which he was member? Of course that church was rightly concerned about proper church order, but any church needs to be more concerned with the evident working of God's Spirit. For that matter, the church of Jerusalem might have considered Philip's right to baptize highly irregular. Indeed, the church sent an apostolic delegation to evaluate the work in Samaria. But the church recognized that questions of church order were subordinate to the authentic marks of God's Spirit. "We ask each other whether we do not sin," said the World Council at Evanston, "when we deny the sole Lordship of Christ over the church by claiming the vineyard for our own, by possessing our ' church ' for ourselves, by regarding our theology, order, history, nationality, etc., as our own ' valued treasures.' " Jesus said, "My sheep hear my voice, and I know them, and they follow me; and I give them eternal life, and they shall never perish, and no one shall snatch them out of my hand." Let us not hinder them.

If the early church had to learn that racial differences must not hinder faith or prevent Baptism, does the church of today not need to learn this? Does the church not sin when it hesitates to receive into its membership the man of darker skin who still asks, "What is to prevent my being baptized? "

Let us return to the doctrinal issue. Someone may say that all of this is true enough of conscious conversion and adult Baptism — but what of the Baptism of infants?

We do not rest the case for infant Baptism on any number of proof texts; we rest it rather on the meaning of Baptism and on the reality of a people of God. To be sure, a trace of the baptismal formula has been seen in the story of Jesus and the children. We read that when parents brought their infants to Jesus so that he might touch them, the disciples sought to forbid them. "But Jesus called them to him, saying, ' Let the children come to me, and do not hinder them; for to such belongs the kingdom of God.' " Nothing is said of Baptism, of course, but the formula, " What hinders? " may be in the mind of the Gospel writer, and the passage was so used in early attempts to validate infant Baptism. Be that as it may, the question remains. What shall the church say to its children? Shall it forbid them Baptism? Shall it assume that there is no such thing as a Christian child? " This does not mean a perfect child," writes Donald Baillie, " for even the most mature Christian on earth is not perfect. And it does not mean a child who has passed through an experience of conversion." And yet, he goes on, is childhood not as much a part of God's plan as are manhood and womanhood? Are children to be outsiders in the church or are they members of the household of faith? " It is His will," Baillie says again, " that so long as they are children they should really be children, and if we do violence to that plan we may turn them into abnormal children who will grow into the wrong kind of adults." If the old Israel included its children in the family of faith through circumcision, shall the new Israel exclude them? " Have you never read," asked Jesus, " ' Out of the mouth of babes and sucklings thou hast brought perfect praise '? "

We are not trying here to renew an old controversy but to suggest that there is a depth of insight in the tradition that we know. Ultimately, the question of Baptism always points us beyond all questions of church order to that Spirit who is not bound by any of our traditions and whose way is so divinely free that " you do not know whence it comes or whither it goes."

" What is to prevent my being baptized? " The question is not asked to frighten me away any more than the question in the marriage ceremony is meant to drive me from my troth. The question is asked so that Christ may reply, " Nothing prevents! " " Forbid them not; for of such is the kingdom of God." This is the word of grace. " To all who received him, who believed in his name, he gave power to become children of God."

The stranger went on his way rejoicing, for he was a stranger no more.

" Come, thou Fount of every blessing,
   Tune my heart to sing thy grace;
Streams of mercy, never ceasing,
   Call for songs of loudest praise."

19

THE WITNESSING CHURCH

"And Jesus came and said to them, 'All authority in heaven and on earth has been given to me. Go therefore and make disciples of all nations, baptizing them in the name of the Father and of the Son and of the Holy Spirit, teaching them to observe all that I have commanded you; and lo, I am with you always, to the close of the age.'"

MATT. 28:18-19

JESUS CHRIST gave his church an endless pledge and an endless task. He told his followers to "wait for the promise of the Father, . . . before many days you shall be baptized with the Holy Spirit . . . and you shall be my witnesses in Jerusalem and in all Judea and Samaria and to the end of the earth." Matthew puts this Great Commission into a baptismal liturgy: "Go therefore and make disciples of all nations, baptizing them in the name of the Father and of the Son and of the Holy Spirit, . . . and lo, I am with you always, to the close of the age." Christ pledges himself to the church "unto the end of the world," and he calls his church "to the end of the earth."

Both the pledge and the task are best expressed in witness — and they are dramatically expressed in the witness of Baptism. The Lord pledges that his church "shall be baptized with the Holy Spirit," and he calls this church "to baptize all nations." That is to say, Christian Baptism is both God's witness to the church and the church's witness to the world.

Baptism is God's witness to the church. Jesus knew that "the

Father who sent me has himself borne witness to me." This witness he heard most clearly in the Voice that came to him in his baptism. "This is the testimony of God that he has borne witness to his Son." As the Father bears witness, so does the Son, for Jesus Christ "fearlessly witnessed to the truth before Pontius Pilate." Again, Christ "gave Himself as a ransom for us all — an act of Redemption which happened once, but which stands for all time as a witness to what He is" (Phillips). So the New Testament calls Jesus Christ "the faithful witness." Moreover, the pledge of God becomes contemporaneous because "the Spirit himself beareth witness with our spirit, that we are children of God." Paul can say as he offers his credentials, "God is my witness."

In Christian Baptism this witness of God becomes visible — the witness of the Father to the Son, the witness of the Son to the redemptive act, and the witness of the Spirit that this redemption is for us. "You shall be baptized with the Holy Spirit," Christ said. It is another way of saying, "Lo, I am with you always, to the close of the age." That is why the gates of hell cannot prevail against the church.

> "And every virtue we possess,
> And every victory won,
> And every thought of holiness,
> Are his alone."

Baptism is God's witness to us.

However, Baptism is also our witness to the world. "Go into all the world and make disciples of all nations, baptizing them in the name of the Father and of the Son and of the Holy Spirit." The church receives the witness of God so that it may witness to the world. "You shall be my witnesses." This is its task. What is the church's witness to the world? It witnesses to God's claim, God's judgment, and God's salvation.

It witnesses to God's claim, for it declares that this is God's world. "Ever since the creation of the world his invisible nature, namely, his eternal power and deity, has been clearly perceived in the things that have been made." The church knows that the world of nature everywhere bears the marks of its Creator and that the world of men everywhere is called to recognize its Lord. In its witness of Baptism, the church calls all men to acknowledge their rightful owner.

Again, the church witnesses God's judgment. "So they are without excuse; for although they knew God they did not honor him as God or give thanks to him, but they became futile in their thinking and their senseless minds were darkened." These are stern words — but true. The church points men to the cross and says, "Behold your God — and behold what you have done to him." Its message is a call to repentance. "Repent, and be baptized every one of you in the name of Jesus Christ for the forgiveness of your sins." The church here follows its Lord who himself came into Galilee, saying, "The time is fulfilled . . . ; repent, and believe in the gospel." In Baptism this witness becomes unequivocal.

Finally, the church witnesses to God's salvation. "Repent therefore, and turn again, that your sins may be blotted out, that times of refreshing may come from the presence of the Lord." Just as its Lord came not to condemn the world but to redeem it, so the church comes not to scold the world but to bring to it God's offer of life. "For the promise is to you and to your children and to all that are far off, every one whom the Lord our God calls to him."

"To all that are far off" — into all the world! "You shall be my witnesses . . . to the end of the earth." The church has no other reason for its existence. Let the church be the church.

> "Baptize the nations; far and nigh
>   The triumphs of the cross record;
> The name of Jesus glorify,
>   Till every kindred call him Lord."

This is our witness, and we must count the cost. God's truth has a cutting edge, and our witness to it can never be measured in popularity or prestige. "Woe to you," warned Jesus, "when all men speak well of you." Significantly, the New Testament word for witness is " martus," which has given us the word " martyr," for witness is costly. Is it any wonder that Jesus Christ should be called " the faithful witness, the firstborn of the dead "? Does the gospel not continually exhort us to witness " unto death "? The early disciples were imprisoned and persecuted, " rejoicing that they were counted worthy to suffer dishonor for the name." One of Mendelssohn's most stirring arias gives powerful expression to this word of the living Christ:

> " Be thou faithful unto death,
>   and I will give thee a crown of life."

Such witness unto death is not confined to the martyrs of the early church, or to the heroes of the Reformation, or to a Kai Munk and Dietrich Bonhoeffer mowed down by Nazi bullets. It can be seen in the embattled Koinonia community of our own South which seeks to express that " in Christ there is no South or North." Witness unto death need not attract the headlines. Whenever and wherever Christians learn what it means to lose themselves for the sake of Christ, that witness is finding expression.

> "Faith of our fathers, holy faith!
>   We will be true to thee till death."

Ought not Christian Baptism to remind us that we are marked men and women? " If any man would come after me, let him deny himself and take up his cross daily and follow me."

Already in present struggle and experience the church knows that the pledge and task of Baptism's witness are true. " After this I looked, and behold, a great multitude which no man could number, from every nation, from all tribes and peoples and tongues, standing before the throne and before the Lamb, clothed in white robes, with palm branches in their hands, crying out with a loud voice, ' Salvation belongs to our God who sits upon the throne, and to the Lamb! ' . . . ' Who are these, clothed in white robes, and whence have they come? ' . . .

' These are they who have come out of the great tribulation; they have washed their robes and made them white in the blood of the Lamb. . . . And he will guide them to springs of living water.' "

In word and sacrament, in worship and life, this vision of the witnessing church begins to find expression. Let the church be the church! Let it be faithful to the seal of its Baptism. Baptized with God's presence, let it go forward to baptize the world.

20

"REJOICE, YE PURE IN HEART"

"Wash me, and I shall be whiter than snow,
Fill me with joy and gladness;
let the bones which thou hast broken rejoice."

Ps. 51:7-8

B LESSED are the pure in heart," said Jesus, "for they shall see God." How can I have purity of heart and wholeness of life?

The psalmist knew. Few hymns have plumbed so deeply the recesses of the heart to find there the springs of God's grace. Few hymns have expressed so well our anxiety and so eloquently God's good news. Little wonder that this psalm has been so deeply woven into the liturgy of Christian faith. Its Kyrie eleison rings with all the deep tones of the New Testament, and its plea for purity finds its answer in Jesus Christ our Lord. Its yearnings have their counterpoint in the glad assurances of Christian sacrament.

Let us listen to the music of Kyrie eleison as Old Testament hymn and New Testament sacrament unite in one glorious fugue of faith.

Kyrie eleison — Lord, have mercy upon us!

> "Have mercy on me, O God,
> according to thy steadfast love; . . .
> Wash me thoroughly from my iniquity,
> and cleanse me from my sin!"

Hymn and sacrament begin here, for there is no other place to begin. Baptism is "for the forgiveness of sins."

> "Foul, I to the fountain fly;
> Wash me, Savior, or I die."

All too well I know that there is no other place to begin.

> "For I know my transgressions, . . .
> Against thee, thee only, have I sinned."

"Repent and be baptized every one of you." Hymn and sacrament and every vital experience of faith know that the judgment of God is true: "So that thou art justified in thy sentence." Jesus once told the story of two men going to worship, and he said that the publican rather than the Pharisee went home justified — for the publican had come in the spirit of Kyrie eleison: "God, be merciful to me a sinner!" Jesus told another story of two brothers, and he said that the prodigal rather than the other entered the Father's house — because the prodigal came in the spirit of Kyrie eleison: "Father, I have sinned against heaven and before you."

> "Against thee, thee only, have I sinned,
> and done that which is evil in thy sight."

At this point, a deeper bass in both hymn and sacrament emphasizes the sense of sin:

> "Behold, I was brought forth in iniquity,
> and in sin did my mother conceive me."

Do not literalize the hymn's poetry or the sacrament's theology into something monstrous. This deeper note of original sin wants to say one thing only — that sin is more than overt act, that it is the pervasive problem that includes us all, that there are no exceptions. As the hymn presses our need for purity back to beginnings, so the sacrament expresses it in infant Baptism.

> "Behold, thou desirest truth in the inward being;
> therefore teach me wisdom in my secret heart."

Not only my actions but my motives need God's cleansing grace — and he is able!

> " Purge me with hyssop, and I shall be clean;
>   wash me, and I shall be whiter than snow."

God is able! The God to whom the heart cries has answered in Jesus Christ: " I will; be clean." He answers still in word and sacrament.

As the hymn comes to the springs of grace, its music changes and the note of joy becomes more evident:

> " Fill me with joy and gladness;
>   let the bones which thou hast broken rejoice. . . .
> " Restore to me the joy of thy salvation,
>   and uphold me with a willing spirit."

Salvation is joy. Jesus said that there is joy in heaven over one sinner that is found. Shall not there be joy on earth? " These things have I spoken to you," he said, " that my joy may be in you, and that your joy may be full." " Rejoice, ye pure in heart! " Such joy is no fleeting moment but becomes a whole new impulse of life:

> " Create in me a clean heart, O God,
>   and put a new and right spirit within me."

Baptism translates this yearning into positive promise, for " if any one is in Christ, he is a new creation." How? There is only one way. God for us must become God in us.

> " Cast me not away from thy presence,
>   and take not thy holy Spirit from me."

Here again yearning becomes assurance in the promise of Baptism that we are God's children " by the washing of regeneration and renewal in the Holy Spirit, which he poured out upon us richly through Jesus Christ our Savior."

The tempo rises and swells in glad dedication:

> " Then I will teach transgressors thy ways,
>   and sinners will return to thee."

The sacrament also knows that salvation is for service, for Baptism is " our engagement to be the Lord's." Faith's music and sacrament point to faith's goal. " My tongue will sing aloud of thy deliverance."

> " Thine wholly, thine alone, I'd live,
>   Myself to thee entirely give."

All this is from the heart, for hymn and sacrament know that no outward ceremonies must ever forget that

> " The sacrifice acceptable to God is a broken spirit;
>   a broken and contrite heart, O God, thou wilt not despise."

" The hour is coming, and now is," said Jesus, " when the true worshipers will worship the Father in spirit and truth, for such the Father seeks to worship him. God is spirit, and those who worship him must worship in spirit and in truth."

Finally, hymn and sacrament are not private concerns but are acts of the worshiping people of God — the church.

> " Do good to Zion in thy good pleasure;
>   rebuild the walls of Jerusalem."

In Old Testament faith God is always " the God of Israel," and in the New Testament " one Lord, one faith, one baptism " belong together. " There is one body and one Spirit, just as you were called to the one hope that belongs to your call."

> " Solid joys and lasting treasure
>   None but Zion's children know."

Well, then, says Paul, " let the word of Christ dwell in you richly, as you teach and admonish one another in all wisdom, and as you sing psalms and hymns and spiritual songs with thankfulness in your hearts to God." We need to sing our faith, for the creed we can sing is the creed by which we can live. The church of Calvin's Geneva sought to express this fundamental insight by singing the Apostles' Creed. After all, if the church triumphant is pictured always as singing a new song before the throne of God, shall not the church on earth also sing its Credo? Let the age-old but ever-new Kyrie eleison sound again in hymn and in sacrament, in worship and in life. " Rejoice, ye pure in heart! "

21

THE SEVENFOLD AMEN

" There is one body and one Spirit, just as you were called to the one hope that belongs to your call, one Lord, one faith, one baptism, one God and Father of us all, who is above all and through all and in all."

EPH. 4:4-6

WE HAVE been trying to suggest the ways in which Christian Baptism interprets and expresses Christian faith. Have we exaggerated? If we as Protestants do not believe Baptism is necessary to salvation but rather portrays this salvation, does it really matter?

The Nicene Creed is cherished by Roman Catholic and Protestant Christians alike, and the Creed wants us to know that Baptism is no mere appendage but an integral part of our Christian faith. "And I believe one holy catholic and apostolic church. I acknowledge one Baptism for the remission of sins." To let go of the seal, the Creed says, would be to scorn what it signifies. Just as the gospel itself is no system of timeless ideas but is ever rooted in the soil of a particular history where the Word was made flesh, so the appropriation of this gospel is no abstract acceptance but is ever expressed in a given, historical sacrament so that the Word may become flesh in our own experience. The sacramental sign is not a mere souvenir but a bequest and a seal by which the living Lord continues to make known who he is and what he is to us.

Here the Creed is faithful to the New Testament, and especially to the Ephesian Letter, which Dr. John Mackay calls

" the distilled essence of the Christian religion, the most au-
thoritative and most consummate compendium of our holy
Christian faith." In a remarkable passage of sustained and exult-
ant music, the apostle embraces the whole gamut of Christian
experience as a sevenfold amen. He has already shown how
God's gracious love has overcome a world of chasmed fears and
deep divisions to create a redemptive order of fellowship " in
Christ." Now, as he exhorts his readers to maintain the unity
that God's love has created, he reiterates the Christian reality in
words that have all the singing quality of a great amen. " There
is *one* body and *one* Spirit, just as you were called to the *one*
hope that belongs to your call, *one* Lord, *one* faith, *one* baptism,
one God and Father of us all, who is above all and through all
and in all."

Here is it — the amen that a divided and distraught world
needs to hear. Here it is — the amen that brings unity where
there has been division, fellowship where there has been rancor,
hope where there has been fear.

Notice that in this great company of spiritual reality, the
apostle gives Baptism a place without any apology. This is all
the more remarkable since Paul does not here include the Supper or the Scripture. " If Baptism was merely a symbol and nothing more," wrote Professor Andrews, " it is difficult to find the
reason which led St. Paul to set it on so high a pinnacle." Why
is Baptism given a place in this sevenfold amen? Is it not the
same reason that finds Baptism in the Creed — because it declares and seals the reality that this faith is *our* faith?

Certainly there is no more appropriate way of concluding
these reflections on Christian Baptism than to let this sevenfold
amen of faith ring out:

> " Let the amen
> Sound from his people again:
> Gladly for aye we adore him."

There is one body. " I believe one holy catholic and apostolic
church." True, the unity of the church is often obscured and

denied by the unhappy fragmentation of a divided Christen-
dom. Sometimes, indeed, it seems almost ludicrous to sing

> " We are not divided,
>   All one body we,
>   One in hope and doctrine,
>   One in charity."

Whittier's lines express a wholesome penitence:

> " Forgive, O Lord, our severing ways,
>   The rival altars that we raise,
>   The wrangling tongues that mar thy praise "

as he pleads that

> " One hope, one faith, one love restore
>   The seamless robe that Jesus wore."

All this is true, yet the unity of the church remains. There is one
body. The communion of saints, the beloved community, is not
something we build by ecclesiastical structures. It is here — if
we but share it and live it and express it in personal and institu-
tional life. Nor is unity to be measured in uniformity. There are
many members, but one body, and " grace is given to each of us
according to the measure of Christ's gift." What is the church?
Says James Smart: " A body of people in whom Jesus Christ
himself lives again to work his works, to speak his words, and to
feed the souls of men."

There is one body. The great church is not organized *out of*
the small ones but *into* them. And Baptism expresses our initiation into this one body. Differing as our several doctrinal and
ecclesiastical traditions may be, it is a significant fact that one
baptismal formula gathers us all together as one body under
one name — " in the name of the Father and of the Son and of
the Holy Spirit."

There is one body because *there is one Spirit*. A body without
a spirit is simply a corpse. " If any man have not the Spirit of
Christ, he is none of his." This is as true of a church as of an

individual. The church is called " the church of the living God " because it has his Spirit. At Pentecost that Spirit created a new community, endowing men with other tongues than the conflicting voices of Babel. Through his Spirit Christ lives in the church, working his works, speaking his words, continuing and completing his gracious redemptive mission — " until we all attain to the unity of the faith and of the knowledge of the Son of God, to mature manhood, to the measure of the stature of the fullness of Christ."

> " Come, Holy Spirit, heavenly Dove,
>   With all thy quickening powers;
> Come, shed abroad a Savior's love,
>   And that shall kindle ours."

And Pentecost still happens and the church still lives — " sealed with the promised Holy Spirit." This the sacrament portrays: " You shall be baptized with the Holy Spirit."

The amen continues, " Just as you were called to the *one hope* that belongs to your call." Paul says, " you . . . were sealed with the promised Holy Spirit, which is the guarantee of our inheritance until we acquire possession of it, to the praise of his glory." The phrase " guarantee of our inheritance " is one of the apostle's continuing themes. Moffatt translates it " the pledge and instalment of our common heritage." This is our Christian hope — we are his. " Beloved," says John, " we are God's children now; it does not yet appear what we shall be, but we know that when he appears we shall be like him, for we shall see him as he is." This is not wishful thinking. This pledge of our inheritance is portrayed in Baptism where God declares that we are his own, to the praise of his glory.

So the amen proceeds, *one Lord*. " The church's one Foundation is Jesus Christ her Lord." " He has made us one," cries Paul. He is the head of the body, " from whom the whole body, joined and knit together by every joint with which it is supplied . . . makes bodily growth and upbuilds itself in love." One Lord — there is no other.

> "The joy of all who dwell above,
>   The joy of all below
> To whom he manifests his love,
>   And grants his name to know."

One Lord — " that at the name of Jesus every knee should bow, in heaven and on earth and under the earth, and every tongue confess that Jesus Christ is Lord, to the glory of God the Father." In its Baptism the church unites to " hail the power of Jesus' name."

One faith, one baptism! This is the faith that binds us together — faith in Jesus Christ as Lord and Savior.

> "Faith of our fathers, holy faith!
>   We will be true to thee till death."

At length the sevenfold amen swells in praise until it encompasses time and eternity " according to the purpose of him who accomplishes all things according to the counsel of his will " — *one God and Father of us all, who is above all and through all and in all.* No Christian affirmation can ever stop short of this ultimate amen. " Blessed be the God and Father of our Lord Jesus Christ, who has blessed us in Christ with every spiritual blessing in the heavenly places, even as he chose us in him before the foundation of the world, that we should be holy and blameless before him." When all is said and done, it is not the love of Jesus that redeems — it is the love of God in Jesus Christ. The cross does not placate an angry deity — " God was in Christ reconciling the world to himself." Yes, blessed be the God and Father of our Lord Jesus Christ. " You cannot experience the grace of Jesus," says James Stewart, " and ever doubt the love of God again. If once at the cross you have seen Christ facing the full force of life's tragic mystery, all the concentrated might of suffering, sin, and death, and conquering in his love, then you know that here is a power which has come forth from the very heart of reality, from the bosom of the Father, and shall yet subdue all things unto itself." This is why the church felt

its earliest baptismal formula — Baptism in the name of Jesus —
was less than complete, and why it very soon adopted the triune
formula which Matthew says has all the force of dominical in-
stitution — " in the name of the Father and of the Son and of
the Holy Spirit." Nothing less will do. Nothing more is possible.

> " Thy children shall not faint nor fear,
>   Sustained by this exalted thought:
>   Since thou, their God, art everywhere,
>   They cannot be where thou art not! "

Well, does not Christian Baptism belong in this sevenfold
amen of Christian faith? If it does belong, let us sound the full
amen:

> " Let the amen
>   Sound from his people again:
>   Gladly for aye we adore him."